I0052725

joining the digital world

how everyone from the complete novice to the expert computer user can use technology to its full potential

www.joiningthedigitalworld.com

Text Copyright © 2007 by Zachary
Hamed

All rights reserved, including the right of
reproduction in whole or in part in any form.

ISBN 978-0-6151-6184-6

Visit the book's website at

www.joiningthedigitalworld.com

Table of Contents

Dedication

To my mother, whose love of pencil and paper and fear of computers spurred me to consider writing this book, and my father, who taught me how to use an old IBM Thinkpad running Windows 95 at the age of 3 and made me the technology lover I am today.

Thanks guys.

ii

Acknowledgments

This book has been two years in the making, and I couldn't have arrived at this point without help from a number of parties.

First and foremost, I would like to thank my parents for edging me on to this point. Even though they were skeptical at the beginning of my writing, they eventually became my largest supporters.

Second, I would like to thank Harry McCracken for writing the introduction to this book.

Third, I would like to thank Collegiate School, Levi, and all other parties that helped in the publication of this, my first, book.

Finally, I would like to thank you, the reader, for supporting my first novel. I hope this endeavor helps you use your technology to a greater extent than before you read this book.

Foreword

Trustworthy tech advice in plain English. That's what we at *PC World* aim to give our magazine readers and web site visitors. And it's also what Zachary Hamed delivers in *Joining the Digital World*—so this is a book very much after my own heart. Zachary does a great job of explaining the basics of computers and providing tips on how to buy the right hardware and software—and he also tells you what to do when things go wrong (which they will—if computers do what they're supposed to reliably, I often tell people, *PC World* may be in trouble).

Time was when some folks were comfortable

with computers and the Internet, and others weren't. Today, of course, being technologically literate isn't optional—it's a necessity of modern life. I happily recommend Zachary's work to anyone who wishes to get all the basics —and more—in a concise, clear, and engaging package.

After almost thirty years as a PC user, and thirteen years working as an editor at *PC World*, I like to think I'm an expert on all this stuff. Even so, I learned new things from this book— and you will, too.

—Harry McCracken

Editor-in-chief of *PC World* Magazine

http://www.pcworld.com/

San Fransisco, California

Please note that the opinions expressed in this introduction are not necessarily shared by the author of this book, and the opinions expressed in this book are not necessarily shared by the author of this introduction.

Part 1

The Nitty Gritty Details

Computers

Computers are complex machines that consist of many smaller components, which in turn work by responding to commands. The basic subunits of these commands are bits and bytes. A bit is an abbreviation of the phrase "**binary digit**". Therefore, it is appropriate to explain the binary number system now.

Binary numbers are an example of a base-2 system; in other words, all numbers, characters, and commands are made up of 2^0, 2^1, 2^2, 2^3, 2^4, 2^5, etc., or 1, 2, 4, 8, 16, 32, etc. However, the computer cannot simply read the number 2 or 8 and create a character. The binary system uses a string of numbers; the first digit from the right represents the number 1, the second from the right represents 2, the third from the right represents 4, the fourth from the right represents 8, the fifth from the right represents 16, and so on. 0s and 1s are used as placeholders, 0 meaning off and 1 meaning on. The computer creates 0s and 1s by sending surges of electricity, 0 meaning electricity off and 1 meaning electricity on. By placing 0s and 1s in different positions, different numbers can be created. By adding the numbers that are presented by the 1s in a binary number string, one can figure out what number the string represents. For example,

00 means 0,

01 means 1,

10 means 2,

11 means 3,

1010 means 10,

1100100 means 100,

And so on and so forth. More zeros can be added to the left of a string of binary numbers. The zeros do not affect the meaning of the string, but by changing the zeros to ones, the meaning changes. Certain binary strings, specifically the strings representing the numbers 1 through 127, also represent every letter, number, punctuation mark, and command you enter into the computer. However, in order to make life for the computer (and the programmer) easier, every binary string representing a number from 1 to 127 is in turn represented by an ASCII code. For example, in the ASCII character set:

A is represented by 65,

B is represented by 66,

C is represented by 67,

a is represented by 97,

b is represented by 98,

c is represented by 99,

A space is represented by 32,

? is represented by 63,

/ is represented by 47,

And so on and so forth. In theory, every character written on the computer should measure one byte, or eight bits. To prove this, open up the Notepad program on a computer running the Microsoft Windows operating system and type a short message. Next, count the number of letters, numbers, spaces, and other characters. The total number of characters and spaces should also be the size of the file in bytes. For example, a file containing the message "new message" should measure 11 bytes, because there are ten letters and one space. However, with the variety of fonts, sizes, and styles available to the word processing user, file sizes vary considerably from the "one byte per character or space" model.

The capacity of computer storage devices such as hard drives and flash drives are measured in groups of bytes. A kilobyte is 1024 bytes, and is usually the smallest measured group of bytes. A megabyte is 1,048,576 bytes, or 1,024 kilobytes. A gigabyte is 1,073,741,824 bytes, or 1,024 megabytes. A terabyte is the largest common measure of bytes, and it is equal to 1,099,511,627,776 bytes, or 1,024 gigabytes.

With this information, we are now adequately prepared to examine the inner mechanisms of the computer.

The motherboard of a computer is analogous to the floor of a kitchen, on which the various appliances rest. In a computer, the motherboard itself is meaningless, but without it none of the components of the computer could work together. The motherboard contains multiple slots for components such as the video, sound, and network cards, the hard drive(s), the memory, and any ports to which peripherals may be added to the computer. Motherboards come in all shapes and sizes, depending on the computer case it is created to fit in. Connected to the motherboard is the brain of the computer, the central processing unit, or CPU. When the computer was invented, there was a universal size for all CPUs. However, as computers became faster, the CPUs needed to grow larger. Therefore, today the two largest CPU manufacturers, Intel and AMD, create various sizes of CPUs depending on their usage; the motherboard's CPU socket is created for the CPU, and for this reason the motherboard is usually bought in accordance with the CPU.

The memory of the computer is divided into multiple parts, three of which are the RAM, the HDD, and the ROM, RAM meaning Random Access Memory, HDD meaning Hard Drive Disk (commonly referred to as "hard drive"), and ROM meaning Read Only Memory. Let's say for a moment the computer was a chef in a kitchen. The chef can place ingredients on the counter in front of him or store them in the freezer. The chef has only a limited amount of space on the counter, but it is faster for him to grab something from there than to retrieve it from the freezer. The freezer is larger with more storage space but is farther away and it takes more time to find food in there than on the countertop. Additionally, the chef can refer to his recipe book, but cannot change the recipes listed in it, whereas he can always put the recipes on the countertop and change them there. In the previous analogy, the counter was parallel to the RAM, the freezer was parallel to the HDD, and the recipe book was parallel to the ROM. RAM is temporary storage, ROM is permanent, non-writable storage, and hard drives are long-term, writable storage. Whenever you create or open a Microsoft Word document, you are actually storing the information temporarily on the RAM until you save the file onto the hard drive. The RAM files are intact and organized, ready for whatever program needs it. Accessing information from the RAM is often faster than accessing it from the hard drive. Downsides of RAM include a higher byte per dollar ratio than hard drives and the fact that once the computer is shut down, information on the RAM is lost. This is why not enabling the automatic saving feature in Microsoft Word or not setting it to save often enough can result in a loss of files and data if the computer shuts down abnormally.

The hard drive, in its simplest form, is a spinning disk on which information is stored. When saving a file, the computer drops small fractions of the file onto various parts of the hard drive while it is spinning. Therefore, one part of your file may be saved in one area while another part is saved in another area. This may seem puzzling, since it is much more difficult to find something if it's broken and the pieces are scattered. Therefore, the hard drive uses a table called the FAT, or the File Allocation Table. The FAT records the locations of the various parts of a file. When you attempt to open a file on your computer, the hard drive uses the FAT to find the various parts of your file and put them together again. Once you save multiple files, the FAT may contain hundreds of thousands of entries; therefore, Microsoft recommends you "defragment" your drive. When you initiate disk defragmentation, the hard drive places the various parts of the file next to each other and reorganizes the entries in the FAT accordingly so it can access the file faster and save you time. Today, hard drives usually contain twenty or more gigabytes of memory, ample space for all the files the average user saves on it. The ROM, one of the other types of memory, is somewhat like a cross between the RAM and the hard drive. The ROM is read only, meaning that the information on it cannot be easily tampered with. The operating system of the computer used to be stored on the ROM, but as operating systems became more sophisticated, the hard drive began to store operating system information. Since hard drives can be formatted by the user, there are many more problems with operating systems today than twenty years ago, mainly because users, viruses, or other external modifiers accidentally or intentionally change the system files, leaving the computer useless unless the operating system is reinstalled.

The memory of the computer completes numerous tasks, one of which is caching. The cache of the computer allows it to access information faster. In order to explain the cache, I'll use the example of a cafeteria. Try to imagine that every time you needed a fork, knife, or spoon, a server had to walk to the end of the serving area (the kitchen) to get your utensils, walk back, and give them to you. With many customers, this process could take time. However, cafeterias, and caches, work differently. Let's say we give the server a tray that can hold utensils. Let's also assume that you use your utensils and bring them back to the server to serve to another customer. If you arrive and ask for a fork, the server must walk to the kitchen, get the fork, and walk back. Once you are done, though, you hand the fork back to the server. Rather than store the fork away, the server keeps it on his tray. When another customer asks for a fork, the server can look at his tray, notice the fork, and serve it to the customer (rather than walk back to the kitchen to retrieve one). Of course, if a customer comes in requesting a spoon, the server still needs to walk to the kitchen. However, the server can place the spoon on his tray, so that any customer who comes in to ask for either a fork or spoon may be served faster. The cache of the computer works in a similar manner. Rather than access information from the hard drive, the RAM, or the ROM, the computer accesses the information from the cache in a period that is typically about two to three times faster than accessing it from the RAM and approximately a thousand times faster than accessing it from the hard drive; reading information from the cache usually takes around twelve nanoseconds, while accessing information from the hard disk takes around twelve milliseconds, an eternity for the CPU that processes information approximately every two nanoseconds. Therefore, different forms of memory and different forms of accessing information hold different roles in the computer.

With this, we conclude our examination of the basics behind the computer. We shall now continue to examine the peripherals that you encounter nearly every time you use a computer.

Peripherals

Computers may be among the most powerful machines invented, yet they wouldn't be so important if nothing they did could be observed, making the computer monitor incredibly useful. Computer monitors and televisions work in similar manners. On computer monitors, images are comprised of pixels, or tiny dots that change color. All colors on a display are created with only 3 pigments: blue, green, and red. All the computer then needs to do is combine various amounts of each in order to display the desired color. By combining various amounts of the 256 shades of red, blue, and green, more than 16 million colors can be produced. The size of monitors varies widely depending on the monitors' intended use.

Computers always output information, but they also need information to be inputed; that is why the computer keyboard and mouse were invented. The design of the modern computer keyboard is based on that of typewriters. The most commonly used keyboard layout is the QWERTY format, which places the letters Q, W, E, R, T, and Y as the first six letters in the first row of alphabetical characters. The other major English format, Dvorak, places the vowels together on one side of the keyboard and the least common letters in the bottom row, the hardest row to reach. Common punctuation marks are located in the top row of the keyboard, and the most common letters are located in the center row. Although the keyboard has a fairly universal format, different companies add and subtract keys to the mix. Computers that natively run Microsoft Windows have a Windows key, which navigates to the Windows start menu. Computers that natively run the Mac operating system have a key with the Apple logo on it, which is a shortcut hotkey to various utilities. Like the computer it is usually connected to, keyboards have a microprocessor and ROM, which interpret the keystrokes you enter. Because of this, you can rearrange the keys on the keyboard even though the computer will still interpret the keystrokes in the QWERTY keyboard layout; conversely, you can reprogram the keyboard to interpret the keystrokes entered into it differently so that various languages may be used to type while using a standard QWERTY keyboard format.

Computer mice are another form of computer input. Currently, there are two major subsections of the computer mouse: the trackball mouse and the optical mouse. Today, the trackball mouse is considered obsolete by most computer users because of its imprecise rubber ball. Trackball mice use two rollers, one for the x axis and one for the y axis. With combinations of movement on both rollers, the computer can determine how much and in which direction to move the mouse pointer on the computer. The optical mouse, today the mouse of choice for millions of computer users worldwide, is divided into two categories as well: laser based and LED (light-emitting diode) based; luckily, both work in similar manners. The laser or light emitted will shine from the mouse, onto the surface, and back to the mouse. This will create an image of the details on the surface on which the mouse scrolls. By taking images many times per second, the mouse can determine how much and in which direction the mouse pointer should move. Optical mice are more precise, do not require a mouse pad to use, and are less prone to dust wear and tear that can damage the precision of a trackball mouse, although optical mice cannot operate on glass or mirrors because the light emitted does not properly reflect back to the mouse. Higher refresh rates, image processing rates, and maximum speeds increase the performance of optical mice.

Today, most mice and keyboards connect to the computer via USB (Universal Serial Bus) ports. USB ports can transmit a maximum of 480 megabits per second. USB 2.0, the newest and most versatile form of USB transmission, allows the connections to change from low transmission for keyboards and mice to medium transmission for printers and scanners to high transmission for high capacity storage systems.

Another transmission medium is Bluetooth. Both mice and keyboards can use Bluetooth technology to wirelessly connect to the computer. Bluetooth technology uses a radio frequency to transmit the information from the mouse and the keyboard to the computer; it does this, however, transmitting only one bit per second, therefore using very little battery power.

Another peripheral you may connect to your computer is the printer. The two main types of printers for personal use are the inkjet and laser, although there are others. Inkjet printers are much cheaper than laser printers. Simply, they operate by applying small dots of cyan (blue), magenta (red), and yellow ink to the paper. By applying these dots, which are only about seven microns (seven millionth of a meter) in length, in different quantities onto the paper in the close vicinity of other colored dots, any color can be created, just like on monitors. Laser printers work quite differently. The toner, or the "ink" of laser printers, is a fine black powder. The powder is applied to a drum, and then applied to the paper. Heated drums then "fuse" the powder to the paper. Laser printers have a higher ppm (page per minute) count than inkjet printers, thereby printing pages out faster; additionally, their toner lasts much longer than inkjet ink.

The CD, or compact disc, is a common form of media distributed in the technology world. A drive reads the CD by shining a laser onto the bottom, shiny side of it. Since the CD is spotted with tiny grooves on the underside, the laser can determine the information stored. Since the grooves are translated into information, scratches can cause the information to be lost or corrupted. You should therefore copy CDs to your computer and backup the information digitally just in case the CD becomes unreadable. CD-R (CD writable) discs can be written on with a CD burner, but are not reusable. CD-RW (CD rewritable) discs can be erased and used again for a limited number of times, and are also written on by a CD burner. Because CDs can only store about 600 megabytes of information, the DVD became another common storage medium, especially for movies. DVDs can store about 4.7 gigabytes of information, and double-sided DVDs can store double that.

Recently there has been much talk of new disc technologies, specifically HD-DVD and Blu-Ray. HD-DVDs can store 15 GB of data per layer and Blu-Ray discs can store 25 GB of data because the laser used is smaller, allowing there to be more grooves on the underside of the disc. Until one of the new formats becomes substantially more popular, you should not invest too much money in either of these new technologies.

The Internet

In its most basic form, the Internet is a group of computers connected together. In fact, when the Internet was created in 1969, it was only a connection between four computers. Today, however, the Internet boats millions of computers and recently reached one hundred million websites. Every computer that is connected to the Internet is connected to a network. Internet Service Providers, or ISPs, provide their customers a network with which the customer may connect to the Internet. However, in order to send information from one network to another, routers are used. Routers receive information, determine where the information is going, and then send it there. Routers can complete the aforementioned process in fractions of a second; that is why you can send an email halfway across the world quite quickly. Each computer has a separate IP address identifying itself. Although you may have a static IP address that never changes, most people have dynamic IP addresses. Dynamic IP addresses are given to your computer by your Internet Service Provider (ISP) when you connect to the Internet and may be taken away when you disconnect. In this manner, the ISP does not have to handle a separate IP address for each customer; rather, it keeps a few that it exchanges. The MAC address of your computer is provided by your ISP and identifies you and your account. Because the MAC address is unique to your machine, many websites use the MAC address rather than the IP address to identify computers.

Only a few years ago, Internet connections were limited to dialup, requiring the computer to use a telephone line to connect. Today, broadband connections are far more common, but speeds can range widely. Keep in mind when looking at Internet connection speeds, however, that there are 8 bits per byte, so you can download a 1 megabyte file in one second (at best) with an 8 megabit per second (mbps) connection; it is a common misconception that mbps is the number of megabytes you can download per second.

URLs label the location of a website or web page on the Internet. The URL begins with HTTP, meaning hypertext transfer protocol, or HTTPS, meaning Hyperlink transfer protocol (secure). It then continues with WWW, meaning World Wide Web, the site's name, then the ending with .com, .org, .net, .edu, or any number of other endings. A slash can be added to the end of the URL, meaning that information after that leads to subsections of the website. Although you do not have to enter the HTTP, HTTPS, or WWW in a URL anymore, they are still added by your browser. Although they might seem like a string of random characters to you, they are very important to the function of the Internet, and unless the Internet is recreated or there is a massive movement of change, the HTTP, HTTPS, and WWW will have to be added at some point during your Internet browsing experience.

Part 2

Tips and Tricks

Password Security

Keeping your data secure can be an annoying process, requiring you to remember countless usernames and passwords. Yet letting your data be compromised by others can lead to headaches far worse than remembering a few letters and numbers. Proper password security is important, but not many people have truly secure passwords. To create a secure password, follow the following steps:

1. Use a password longer than six characters.
2. Use both capital and lowercase letters.
3. Use numbers, letters, and other characters such as periods, underscores, etc.
4. Do not write down your password.
5. Do not tell your password to anyone.
6. Do not use easily available personal information such as a pet's name, birthday, child's name, etc.
7. Try not to use real words in the password. Hackers regularly use a dictionary to enter possible passwords, so if your password is an actual word, it can be easily hacked. Any intended misspelling of a word is just as obscure to a hacker and the dictionary as a slew of random characters, so try misspelling a word in a way you can remember. You can also try alternating between the spellings of two words.

For example, combine cat and dog to get the following: cDaOtG.

8. Change your password every 3 months or so.

General Internet Security

1. Do not click on the links or download the attachments in emails if the email is suspicious in any way. It is possible to write a URL that links to an address different than that specified, possibly opening a malicious site. Malicious attachments downloaded to your computer can complete any number of tasks, such as deleting critical system files, sending sensitive personal information to third parties, etc.

2. Referring back to the previous tip, not all emails are what they seem. I have experiences in which I have received emails with an authentic eBay email address that told me my account had been compromised and that I should change my password by entering my old password and username. Before I did so, I checked on eBay's site and was told eBay never contacts you via email asking for that kind of personal information. The moral of this story? Check on the company's website before answering any emails appearing to be sent from them.

Referring back to the previous tip, if your bank sends you an email, do not click on the link to your account. Doing so may lead you to a fake website with a URL one character off the actual website that looks like the actual site, run by people trying to get your login information.

3. To go to a website in which you intend to login, search for the site on Google. The first result is usually the authentic site, and doing so diminishes the risk that you will type the URL incorrectly, leading you to a fake website trying to get your information.

4. Ensure the page you're entering your information into is secure. In Firefox, a yellow lock should appear to the right of the URL and/or the URL should start with "https" rather than "http".

5. Use a good Internet security suite. My recommendation is ClamWin, since it is free and doesn't slow down your computer with constant popups.

eBay Security

eBay is an online auction site that allows users to post items for sale so other users can bid on them. However, there are many fake buyers and sellers that try to cheat you out of your money. To stay safe on eBay, follow the following tips:

1. Check a seller's feedback rating. The higher a percentage it is, the more positive reviews he or she has received. Keep in mind, though, that there are con artists that truthfully sell products to get a positive rating, then try to sell expensive items with the positive rating and cheat buyers at that point.

2. If the offer is too good to be true, it is. Some people sell new laptops that usually retail for thousands of dollars for a few hundred. In those cases, do not attempt to bid for the item. The seller will likely take your money and run.

3. Never use money order to pay for an item, and never agree to meet a seller in person unless you're sure he or she is not a threat to you. Always use Paypal to pay for items on eBay.

4. Use your discretion when buying items on eBay, as some things can't logically be bought without seeing them in person. Laptop computer? Sure. An authentic cannon used in the American Revolution? Probably not.

5. Be weary about sellers from other countries. eBay cannot interfere in the sale of products from certain countries, so be careful what you buy because there may not be any assurances

from eBay.

6. The seller usually calculates shipping for the item, tells you what service he or she will use, and then states how much it will cost. Calculate the price for shipping and see if it matches the seller's price. If the seller posted an egregiously high price, tell eBay.

7. Don't be afraid to ask questions about the product to the seller. If he or she doesn't answer you in a timely or respectful manner, don't even bother buying from him or her.

8. Bidding at the last minute is a good way to snag items cheaply, but if you hedge your bets too many times you may lose the auction.

Buying a New Computer

If you're buying a new computer, you may be confused regarding what you really need. If so, use the following guide:

Are you a music, photo, graphics, or video professional?

Buy a Mac.

Are you a very basic computer user, using the computer only to browse the web, check email, etc.?

Buy a Dell running Ubuntu Linux.

Are you a mobile user and find it useful to be able to move your computer?

Plan on buying a laptop.

Are you positive you won't need or want to move your computer?

A desktop computer is for you. Desktops are generally cheaper and offer more horsepower than comparable laptops.

Good Computer Brands

Some brands offer computers that are better deals, more powerful, or lighter. Here is a description of some of the better computer brands:

1. HP

HP's line of computers used to focus on business machines, but it recently revamped its line with powerful, cheap, and modern laptops and desktops. The laptop line has a wide range of screen sizes, applying to many different types of users. HP's desktops are more geared towards entertainment uses, since they have bright, large screens and some are even touch-sensitive.

2. Fujitsu

Fujitsu's line of computers is slightly more expensive than the lines of other computer companies, but their laptops are also considerably lighter than the competition. Users who need a light, thin, and small laptop and do not take price greatly into consideration should look no further than Fujitsu.

3. Acer

Acer's line of both desktops and laptops are cheap but not very powerful. They are geared to the more casual computer users, although the Rolls-Royce of their laptop line is the Acer Ferrari laptop series. The computers are fast and modern with Ferrari style in mind, although they are also very expensive.

4. IBM/Lenovo

IBM is almost certainly not a personal computer company, but its focus on business computers clearly shows. Their laptops are durable, lightweight, and small, so they are perfect for users who travel a lot, and the desktops are made for businesses. Lenovo recently bought IBM's computer division, so all new IBM laptops will have a Lenovo company logo rather than IBM's, but the computers are just as good.

5. ASUS

ASUS makes good gaming laptops, but they also have a Lamborghini laptop line that has leather placed where the hands rest when typing and are very fast, streamlined, and expensive.

6. Dell

Dell's laptops are very basic and cheap, but for a long time were also bland and gray. They recently updated their line with more colorful choices, allowing consumers to choose colors such as black, white, blue, red, green, yellow, pink, and brown. Their laptops are good desktop replacements, but are generally not good for carrying around. The XPS line, Dell's gaming line, is the exception to that rule, since some of them are light enough to comfortably carry around.

7. Apple

Apple's laptops are arguably the best looking computers on the market. Because both the hardware and software were created by the same company, they work seamlessly together. The problem is, Apple's operating system is very closed, has very few outside applications, and is not customizable to the extent Microsoft Windows is. The computers' components are overpriced and there are very few options that you can customize when building your computer.

Buying a Laptop

Are you:

Going to Use the laptop for very basic computing and run only one or two applications at a time?

> You need a minimum of 512 MB of memory, and a dual core processor is not a necessity.

Going to use the laptop for business or games, or regularly run three or more programs at a time?

> You need a minimum of 1 GB of memory, and a dual core processor.

Going to travel with your laptop frequently?

> Get a laptop that weights less than 5 pounds and with a 14 or less inch screen. Otherwise, ignore weight and screen size, and buy a light or heavy laptop with a large or small screen as you deem appropriate.

Computer Accessories

There are some computer accessories that you need regardless what computer you buy. First, buy an external drive that is at least double the amount of storage space you have on your computer. Use this drive for daily backups of your information. Second, get a power strip with built in surge protector. Power surges can literally crash your computer and lose thousands of your files (though this tip is more important for desktop users than laptop users). Finally, an optical mouse, if you didn't receive one with your computer, is a must.

Windows XP, Windows Vista, Mac OS X, Leopard, and Linux: What's the Difference?

The two leaders in the operating system market, Microsoft and Apple, have two different operating systems. Making a decision about what operating system to buy can be difficult, since the choice will directly affect your computing experience. I have very strict views about which operating system is best, opinions I will share below.

Microsoft's Windows operating system was the created for the business environment, and until XP Windows was a delicate balance between the operating system for the home user and that for the business user. Today, Windows Vista is Microsoft's newest operating system and is a near perfect balance between work and play. There are disadvantages to Vista, however, as you will read below.

Apple's Mac OS X is a relatively new operating system that was a huge jump from previous versions of the Mac operating system. The operating system is not available separate from a computer, so you have to buy a Mac to get Mac OS X.

Leopard is Apple's newest operating system. It boasts a few new features, including the ability to go back in time with your computer's data to retrieve an old file and the ability to view files without actually opening them, most of which are already available in Windows Vista or with third party programs.

I am 100% behind Windows for several reasons. First, Windows is easily customizable, especially with the Registry Edit option. Next, it is true that Windows gets viruses, but it is only a matter of time until Macs get viruses as well, since Windows gets so many viruses because it is still the most popular operating system. In a lot of ways, Macs are more prone to viruses because their wireless networking option is on by default, an easy way for hackers to take control of the computer. Next, Apple has a tight grip on its computers, voiding your warranty if you add extra

RAM and charging extremely high prices for computer components. Although Macs come ready right out of the box with software for music, photos, and video, Windows lets you choose what programs you want since there are so many freeware, shareware, and donationware programs that run on Windows. Even though you can run both Windows and Mac OS X on a Mac, why bother when you can get a cheaper, better, probably faster PC running Windows? Next, nearly all of the programs on the Mac operating system have parallel programs that have equal or better value and quality. The one feature on the Mac that draws people in is the eye candy, with the glossy screen, icons, and overall clean interface. If you are a music, photo, graphic, or video professional, go ahead and get Mac OS X. But sometimes functionality beats beauty, and if you want to actually do something with your computer, use Windows. Windows is as simple or complicated as you want it to be, making it a very generic operating system catering to a huge swatch of the computer market.

Linux is a free alternative to Windows that only a few years ago was usually only used by computer experts and professionals, especially on Internet servers. Ubuntu Linux then reinvented Linux's image by making it simple enough for the home user. If you use your computer for very basic uses such as word processing, checking email, and browsing the Internet, consider using Ubuntu on an old PC. Certain Dell computers now have the option of having Ubuntu installed natively, meaning you don't have to install it and you save $100 or more that usually goes to Microsoft for Windows. If you are a regular computer user and have Windows XP or Vista installed, don't switch to Ubuntu. But if you are buying a new computer and don't need anything fancy or have an old computer running Windows 2000 or below that you want to use, Ubuntu is a great option.

So what's the difference between Windows XP and Vista? If you have a computer that runs XP, don't update to Vista unless you really want the improved Aero graphics interface and your computer can run it (you need a good 1 GB of RAM): wait for the first Vista Service Pack to come out before switching (though the status of a Vista Service Pack is currently unavailable from Microsoft). If you're planning on buying a new computer, don't worry about Vista, especially with the issue of program compatibility. All programs I have installed on Vista have worked perfectly; there are some programs that are not Vista compatible, so if there is a particular program you *must* use, check on the software's website to ensure it is Vista compatible. Overall, I am very happy with Windows Vista and its new features. Among the new features is ReadyBoost, which allows you to add RAM to your computer by adding a flash drive or memory card, helpful when your computer has less than 1 GB of memory and you want to add more without paying too much. Keep in mind before you do this, however, that adding a flash drive or memory card with a slow read and write speed can actually slow down your computer, so get high speed memory or drives that are optimized for ReadyBoost.

If you're confused about the four versions of Vista, don't be. Basically, Microsoft created four versions of Vista targeted at four different groups of buyers: the very basic computer user who does not need (or whose computer cannot handle) fancy graphics (Vista Basic Edition), the average computer user who wants (and whose computer can handle) fancy graphics (Vista Home Premium Edition), the business user (Vista Business Edition), and the user who can afford to shed out a few more bucks for a few more benefits (Vista Ultimate Edition). If you buy a computer with more than 1 GB of memory, get Home Premium, since the graphics are a welcome bonus. Vista Business adds security features, so if you use your laptop for business, Vista Business should be your choice. If you have the money to spend on the Ultimate Edition, go for it. It has a few extra features (which you should check out before you buy it) that make it worth the higher price.

So in conclusion, if you:

Have Windows XP,

> Keep it until the first Vista Service Pack is released unless you love the new graphics Vista offers.

Are buying a new computer with 1 GB or more of RAM,

> Get any version of Vista but Vista Basic.

Are buying a new computer with less that 1 GB of RAM,

> Get Vista Basic.

Are a Very Basic Computer User,

> Get a Dell with Ubuntu.

Are a Music, Photo, Graphics, or Video Professional,

> Get a Mac running Mac OS X.

Best and Worst Programs for (Nearly) Everything

Please note that any spaces appearing in the following website links are actually underscores (_).

Best word processing suite: OpenOffice.org

http://www.openoffice.org/

OpenOffice is an open source word processing suite for Microsoft Windows, Mac OS X, and some Linux kernels. It has many, if not all, of the features found in Microsoft Office, and those who are accustomed to Microsoft Office's feel and layout will quickly adjust to OpenOffice. OpenOffice comes in a suite that contains word processing, spreadsheet, presentation, and database programs, but also includes two programs that Microsoft Office does not include: a drawing program and a Math Type program for writing complicated math equations on the computer. Overall, this is my favorite suite because of its integration between programs and its price.

Best painting program: The GIMP

http://www.gimp.org/

The GIMP is a free program for Windows, Mac OS X, and various Linux kernels. It is helpful with more complicated picture editing, such as adjusting the opacity of colors, creating color gradients, patterned backgrounds, etc. If you need a simpler painting program, use Microsoft Paint.

Best (simple) photo editing software: Picasa

http://picasa.google.com/

Picasa is a personal favorite of mine, since it combines both simple and advanced features in a layout that the user can understand almost immediately. It has the ability to correct the infamous red eye, adjust brightness and contrast, and crop photos. It also has the "I'm Feeling Lucky" option, which allows Picasa to automatically fix what it thinks are problems in the picture (brightness, contrast, red eye, etc.) Often, this feature allows a one click fix to all the common photo issues; other times, however, Picasa's choices are not desirable, yet they can always be undone.

Best online mapping service: Google Maps

http://maps.google.com/

Google Maps allows the user to enter an address anywhere in the world and view a map of the specified area. It also gives directions to locations, offers aerial views, shows areas where there is traffic in real-time, allows you to view the location from the street (Google Street View), and more. It's easier to use than Mapquest, more customizable, and more user-friendly.

Best global imaging program: Google Earth

http://earth.google.com/

Google Earth is a compilation of aerial views of the entire world; many news agencies use the paid version of this program to show aerial pictures of countries to the public. The free version allows the user to explore any part of the globe, and the image quality is remarkable. There is currently no program available online that reaches the caliber, quality, and simplicity of Google Earth.

Best web browser: Mozilla Firefox (Most recent version)

http://www.mozilla.com/en-US/firefox/

Mozilla Firefox is a fairly new web browser, comparable to Microsoft's Internet Explorer and the Opera browser. Mozilla offers several features ahead of its time, such as an integrated RSS reader, tabbed browsing, security features, toolbar views, and seamless integration with its sister email program, Mozilla Thunderbird. I find that it offers faster performance than Internet Explorer, but there are still people who prefer Internet Explorer over Firefox.

Best downloadable email client: Mozilla Thunderbird

http://www.mozilla.com/en-US/thunderbird/

Mozilla Thunderbird allows you to incorporate numerous email accounts from various email providers into one program. It works together seamlessly with Mozilla Firefox, and, once set up, is very easy to use.

Best online email service: Gmail and Litepost

http://gmail.com/

http://litepost.com/

http://mail.litepost.com/?m=login/

Gmail offers a lot of storage for emails, but is admittedly not the easiest service to use. If you are comfortable using Gmail, I strongly recommend it. If you feel that you just want to create and send emails without any fancy interface, use Litepost. Registration is free and easy, and the interface is streamlined, simple, and eye-catching. Only basic email options (create, send, read, and forward emails, reply to an email, attach files to an email, and search through your emails) are listed in order to minimize confusion, making it my choice for the basic or beginner email user. The second link above allows you to read about

Litepost, while the third link allows you to sign up for an account.

Best search engine: Google

http://www.google.com/

Google is now a household name, even a recognized word by certain dictionaries. Google's simplicity attracts novice users, yet the algorithms behind it are fairly complicated. For more information on Google and its services, see pages 88-99.

Best VoIP (Voice Over IP) program: Skype

http://skype.com/

Skype is the market leader in the VoIP sector, and fairly so. It has seamless integration with video chats and instant messaging and offers free, good quality calls between computers and calls to and from landlines and cell phones for a small fee. It can serve as a decent security system with some webcams, and it is also a way to talk with (and see) relatives across the country or across the world for free.

Best (free) CD burner software: Infrarecorder and Burn

http://infrarecorder.sourceforge.net/

http://burn-osx.sourceforge.net/

Infrarecorder for Windows and Burn for Mac OS X are the best open source versions of CD burning software of their respective sectors. They're easy to use and offer features not found even in their commercial counterparts.

Best (free) Windows music and video player: Windows Media Player (Most recent version)

http://www.microsoft.com/windows/windowsmedia/

Windows Media Player has come packaged with versions of Windows for years. Its integration with the Windows operating system makes it the choice of many music and video enthusiasts.

Best Mac OS X music and video player: iTunes

http://www.apple.com/itunes/

No surprise here; iTunes is the leader in music and video players for the Mac operating system. It is largely known as a gateway to Apple's iPod, but it is also a surprisingly good player for music and videos bought on iTunes for viewing on the computer. I do not extend this recommendation to the community of Windows users who do not have an iPod, however, because there are better alternatives (for example, Songbird and Windows Media Player).

Online Tools

Track the Price of an Airline Ticket

http://www.yapta.com/

Assuming you bought an airline ticket, simply enter your flight number and **Yapta** will tell you if and when the price of your ticket rises or falls. You can then get vouchers or a refund if the price of the ticket falls before you travel. Additionally, you can use **Yapta** before you buy a ticket so you can get a decent price.

Find the Best Time to Buy Airline Tickets

http://www.farecast.com/

Sometimes waiting one or two days before you travel can save you hundreds of dollars, and planning in advance can save you even more. **Farecast** tries to help you save by graphing the expected airline rates and forecasting when would be the best time to travel, depending on whether fares are rising, steady, or falling presently. It also allows you to see how long you should stay at your destination, since staying an extra day could save you money as well.

Look at Old Versions of Websites

http://www.archive.org/web/web.php/

The Internet today is full of valuable information, but sometimes the need to see a version of a website at a certain point in the past arises. **The Wayback Machine** has archived more than 85 billion web pages from 1996 to a few months from the date of access. Type in almost any famous or small website, and you can see the changes it had over time. For example, search for Google to see the site when Sergey Brin and Larry Page first launched it, or search for CNN to see what the headlines were in 2000.

Estimate the Gas Necessary for a Trip by Car

http://www.fuelcostcalculator.com/

With fuel costs rising, it is often helpful to know whether driving is cheaper than another form of transportation and how much money will be spent on gas. If you don't want to do the calculations, the **AAA's Fuel Cost Calculator** allows you to plan your trip and calculate the fuel usage based on your car's make and model beforehand so you can save money.

Get a Hassle-Free Temporary Email Address

http://www.mailinator.com/

Nearly every website now needs you to register to access it, and most registrations need to send a confirmation email. The same sites may then send emails to you that you never asked for, filling your inbox needlessly. Therefore, temporary email addresses were created to receive an unimportant email, say, a confirmation email from a website you recently registered with, and then expire so the email address can be reused. The problem with most temporary email addresses is that you have to open a new window, register for an account, and then continue with your registration. Instead, you can use **Mailinator**. Make up any email you wish ending in "@mailinator.com" (for example, exampleemail@mailinator.com). Supply the website asking for an email address with the email you just thought of, and then go to mailinator.com and login by entering the email address you made without the need for a password (it's a temporary mailbox). The email you sent will be there, you never had to register at mailinator.com, and you didn't have to remember a password.

Use Virtually Any Search Site Quickly

http://www.sputtr.com/

Google is the Swiss Army knife of search engines, but sometimes other websites are more suitable for a certain search. Therefore, **Sputtr** allows you to search Google, Yahoo, Windows Live Search, Ask, Amazon, eBay, Wikipedia, Digg, Reddit, Facebook, YouTube, CNET, and other sites by entering a search term and clicking on the desired site's logo, a process that can take as little as five seconds. Keep it bookmarked for a fast browsing experience.

Create a Photo Flipbook with Music

http://www.jumpcut.com/

A photo slidehshow is all well and good to send to friends and family, but sometimes adding music makes the slideshow more captivating. No online tool is easier to use and more professional looking than **Jumpcut**. Sign up for an account, upload the photos and music you want to use, specify how fast you want the photos to flip by, and publish it on their website. Send the URL to loved ones to share your memories!

Turn Your PC into a Photobooth

http://www.cameroid.com/

Macs come preinstalled with Photobooth, software that allows you to use the integrated webcam to take warped, nostalgic, and often funny pictures. Most PCs do not come with software up to par with Photobooth, so PC users can use the online tool **Cameroid** to take pictures. There are many options that promise hours of fun, and some options are not included with Macs, making it a good tool for both Mac and PC users.

Edit Photos Online

http://www.phixr.com/

You don't need to buy expensive software to edit photos expertly. Use **Phixr** to edit your photos online, on any computer.

Find New Music, Tailored to Your Tastes

http://www.pandora.com/

The **Pandora Music Project** is an Internet radio project that allows you to enter a song that you especially like and, although it may or may not play the song, the software will identify the musical qualities in the track and will then play free songs that have similar qualities. It is a great way to find new music that you like, and is entirely legal.

Open Source Software Directory

http://www.osalt.com/

Open source software generally allows you to view the source code of the software and distribute copies for non-commercial use, and is usually free. There are often several free alternatives to almost every commercial software available, but it is sometimes difficult to find them. **Osalt** therefore chronicles alternatives to paid software such as Microsoft Access, Apple Final Cut Pro, and other programs. It is a great way to save money and get equal or greater functionality out of your computer.

Online Time Tracker for Freelancers

http://www.toggl.com/

Tracking billable hours for customers is a difficult job for freelancers, and recording what jobs were done for different periods of time can require the organization of numerous records. Therefore, **Toggl** allows you to enter a job name, start and stop a timer that remembers how long you worked on each job, enter a price for different jobs, and print an invoice for the total price owed and detailing the price for each individual job.

Online Budget Management

https://www.moneytrackin.com/

Rather than buy expensive budget management
software, you can use **Moneytrackin'**, a free site that
allows you to budget your money easily, manage
different accounts, and track and graph income and
expense over time.

Find Mailboxes in Your Area

http://www.mailboxmap.com/

Sometimes you need to drop your mail off in a blue
USPS mailbox in your area, but do not know where
the closest one is. **Mailbox Map** allows you to enter an
address to find the nearest mailbox.

Check the Actual Speed of Your Internet Connection

http://internetfrog.com/mypc/speedtest/

Internet providers often promise a certain Internet
speed, but how do you reliably know that you're
getting the speed promised? Visit the **Online Speed
Test** from InternetFrog and it will tell you your upload
and download speed and how long it would take you
to download a 1, 10, and 100 megabyte file.

Netflix for Books

http://www.bookswim.com/

Netflix has changed the movie renting industry forever, but those who are of the literary type will appreciate **Bookswim**, which is basically Netflix for books. You specify which books you want to receive, get them in the mail, and return them whenever you want with no late fees. Prices currently begin at $23.99 a month.

Convert Video for Use on Handheld Devices

iPods and other handheld devices sometimes do not accept the file format you wish to transfer to it. Therefore, use **3gp converter** to convert various video formats into formats compatible with iPods, Playstation Portables (PSPs), and other devices. Since 3GP is easily downloaded from a number of online sites, search for "3GP Converter" on Google to find a download source.

Talk to a Human in Customer Service Without Navigating Phone Trees

http://www.nophonetrees.com/

http://www.ivrhacks.com/

Phone calls to customer service can be long and

aggravating, especially since one wrong button press can mean making another call and staying on the phone for hours waiting for an available agent. **BRINGO** navigates the phone trees for you, and then calls you back at a user provided number when it navigates the phone tree, meaning you don't have to stay on the line. You can also use **IVR Hacks** to navigate phone trees by visiting the website, clicking the desired company, and following the on-screen directions.

Give a Link, Not an Email

http://www.contactify.com/

In some situations, especially on web forums of which spammers are members, giving out your personal email is not a good idea. Even though some people legitimately want to contact you, others want to send unsolicited messages to your inbox, which can sometimes get out of hand. **Contactify** tries to take away the risk of contacting others online by creating a link which you can post on the web. When the link is pressed, users are led to a contact form that does not reveal your email address, but instead lists the messages on the Contactify site, meaning emails are not forwarded to your inbox.

Create Your Own Icons

http://converticon.com/

If you want to replace the pictures that appear as shortcuts on your desktop with your own pictures, use **ConvertIcon**. Simply convert your picture to PNG format (open it in Microsoft Paint and save the file in the PNG format) and upload it to the **ConvertIcon** website. It will then convert the picture to the ICO format that is used for icons and allow you to download it.

Get Free Icons

http://www.iconfinder.net/

If you don't want to make your own icons, **IconFinder** has a collection of over 20,000 fabulous icons that are free to download.

Find Wireless Signals Around Town

http://www.wefi.com/

If you're traveling to an area of town you're not familiar with, use **WeFi**. **WeFi** allows users to look at the signal strength of various hotspots that both require and do not require a password. You can also add signals you encounter so other users can find them. Sometimes moving a block or two can give you a faster, stronger connection, making **WeFi** a good tool for users on the go.

Use an Online Desktop

http://www.goowy.com/index.aspx/

If you don't carry a laptop around, online desktops are the next best thing. They provide similar functionality to normal desktops, albeit a little watered down, but can be accessed anywhere you have an Internet connection. **Goowy** is my personal favorite online desktop, but there are several available. Create an account with **Goowy**, and you can access the Internet, play games, check your email (**Goowy** offers its own email as well), use the file storage option, instant message, use the calendar and RSS reader, and more.

Use One Telephone Number, Not Ten

http://www.grandcentral.com/

If you have more than one telephone that you alternate between, you can use **GrandCentral**, a free service recently bought by Google, to get just one number. You pick your area code, and **GrandCentral** will give you one number that will forward any incoming call to your other telephone numbers. You can therefore choose which phone you want to pick up (helpful if you're conserving your wireless minutes) and you'll never miss a call even if you're not near one particular telephone.

Find Great, Free Children's Stories

http://www.childrensbooksonline.org/index.htm

Many children's stories are timeless classics, but you can end up spending hundreds of dollars on books that your child may only read once or twice. To read or download children's books, visit the **Children's Books Online** site, sponsored by the Rosetta project. It has a collection of hundreds of books, some of which are audiobooks. They also categorize the books by age, helpful when trying to find just the right story for your little one.

Find New Music

http://www.musicmesh.net/

If you want to find new music similar to music you've heard, check **MusicMesh**. It allows you to search for music you know, and then creates a graphic organizer of other music similar to the one you searched for, complete with reviews from other users, a track list, song previews for certain songs, Wikipedia entries, and the Amazon listing for the album.

Get Free eBooks (Legally)

http://www.gutenberg.org/wiki/Main_Page/

For the largest selection of public domain eBooks, check out **Project Gutenberg**. With more than 20,000 books, you're bound to find a few you've always wanted to read.

Get Free Audiobooks (Legally)

http://www.librivox.org/

Audiobooks are a great way to catch up on literature on the go, but most people pay for them. **Librivox** lets you download, for free, books in the public domain. The catch? Volunteers, who may or may not be professional orators, read the books. But **Librivox** has such a large selection that you'll quickly forget that the speakers are volunteers. If you're so inclined, you can volunteer to read as well.

Easy File Uploads

http://upload.divshare.com/

For easy and free file hosting, use **Divshare**. It uploads files very quickly, lets you upload up to 200 MB at a time, and they say they'll host the files forever. You can share the files as well.

Get Price Comparisons From Your Phone

http://www.frucall.com/

If you want to find out whether you're getting a good price for virtually anything in a store, dial 1-888-DO-FRUCALL or 1-888-363-7822, enter the product's barcode or ISBN number, and **Frucall** will tell you the best prices online, and will even let you buy from merchants directly on your phone.

Send a Video Email

http://www.eyejot.com/

If you want to send video emails to friends and family without downloading any software, use **Eyejot**. It allows you to record and send video emails to any email addresses for free. Although the message length is limited to sixty seconds, that's generally more than enough time to communicate what you want, and you can always send more than one.

Send Emails Easily on the Go

http://www.jott.com/

If you want to send emails on the go but don't have the proper application to do so, use **Jott**. Register for **Jott**, call 1-877-568-8486, and **Jott** will ask you to whom you would like to send an email, ask you to dictate your message, and then let you hang up. **Jott** will take your words and use speech recognition software to create an email and send it to the proper recipients. **Jott's** speech recognition is spectacular, and although it limits you to 30 seconds of speaking, it is extremely helpful when you have to send an email to one or more people and cannot type it.

Organize Your Family Online

http://www.cozi.com/

If you want to keep all members of your family on the same page, use **Cozi**. It allows you to create calenders, exchange messages, create shopping lists, and more, either from the Internet or from a downloadable application. It also allows you to send text message reminders to your family members' phones.

Scan Documents with Your Digital Camera or Cameraphone

http://www.scanr.com/

If you want to scan documents on the go, use **ScanR**. Take a picture of a document, upload the picture, and specify an email address, and **ScanR** will email you with a PDF of the information you took a picture of. Although the scanning quality is a bit spotty, it is still a great way to scan a document when you don't have a scanner nearby.

Mapquest for Public Transportation

http://www.publicroutes.com/

If you want to know how to get from Point A to Point B using public transportation, use **Public Routes**. Enter the start and end addresses, and it will tell you how to get there using trains and buses. It's currently available for 17 US cities (including New York) and London, so it's a great way to avoid traffic.

Print Out Calendars, Graph Paper, Sudoku Puzzles, and More

http://www.pdfpad.com/

The title says it all. Only at **PDFPad**.

Print Out Your Own Business Cards

http://www.businesscardland.com/home/

If you want to print out simple but professional looking business cards on your own computer, check out **Businesscardland**. Enter your information, choose the colors and design, and print out 10 cards per page.

Get the Most Hotel Points for Your Trip

http://www.pointmaven.com/

If you have several hotel rewards cards and want to find the one that will offer the most hotel rewards points, **PointMaven** will help you do just that. Enter the location you're traveling to, and **PointMaven** will list hotel promotions for several popular hotel rewards programs so you can get the most points for your trip.

Get the Best Deals from Amazon

http://www.junglecrazy.com/

For all the items on Amazon that are 70% off or more, go to **JungleCrazy**. The huge list has a number of great buys that you probably wouldn't find otherwise.

Social Networking for...Moms?

http://www.opmom.com/

Mothers might be the group of people most likely to benefit from social networking, so its no wonder **OpMom** is such a popular service, not only in the United States but also internationally.

A Better Online TV Guide

http://couchville.com/guide/

TV Guide may be a good magazine, but its online guide is decently bad. **Coucheville** improves upon TV Guide by letting you pick your location and drag through the listings, much like you do with Google Maps. Its easier, faster, and more functional than TV Guide's website.

Real Time Weather—Right Down to the Block

http://www.weather.com/weather/map/interactive/

If you want to see the weather anywhere in the U.S., live, for free, and right down to the block level, **the Weather Channel** offers an excellent tool that shows real-time weather radar across the country.

Get Free Drawing Lessons Online

http://dev.drawspace.com/

Getting a professional artist to teach you how to draw could cost thousands of dollars, but that's exactly what Brenda Hoddinott, the owner of **Drawspace,** is doing. By classifying her lessons into three categories (beginner, intermediate, and advanced) and sharing them online, she ensures anyone can learn how to draw easily with some hard work and repetition.

Find Out How Much a Site is Worth

http://www.dnscoop.com/

If you've ever wondered how much a site is worth and could be sold for, **dnScoop** is the tool that does just that. It uses several variables, including number of visitors and the amount of advertising revenue. How much is Google worth? At the time of publication, $1,743,760,000.

Child-Friendly Freeware

http://www.kaboose.com/

To get programs targeted for children, as well as health, food, crafts, and other tips, check out **Kaboose**.

Figure Out What Congress Is Doing

http://www.opencongress.org/

If you want to get involved in government and see what bills Congress is passing, **OpenCongess** is just what you need. It lists the bills Congress is passing, what they concern, information on congressmen and women, and more. It's a great way to keep tabs on what your elected officials are doing without attending every congressional meeting.

Get Subway Maps for International Locations for Free

http://www.amadeus.net/home/new/subwaymaps/en/
index.htm#

It's sometimes difficult to find good quality subway maps online. Visit the above address to get subway maps for a number of locations around the world for free. The maps are large and relatively easy to read, and are great to find your way around town.

Replace your iPod's battery

http://www.ipodjuice.com/

http://www.ipodhowtovideo.com/

Apple's battery replacement program, like everything else the company offers, is horribly overpriced. You pay more than $60 for a battery that doesn't last a year. To do the job yourself (which isn't that hard but will most likely void your warranty), visit the above websites. The first lets you buy an iPod battery replacement kit that gives you all the tools you need for less than half the price of Apple's battery program. The second site has video tutorials showing you how to go about replacing the battery.

Create a Comic Strip from Your Photos

http://www.pikistrips.com/home/

Sometimes photos would look great in a comic strip, and a comic strip is often a great way to send friends and family pictures of vacations, babies, etc. **PikiStrips** makes it easy to create comic strips and share them with your friends.

Excel and Calculator—Merged

http://instacalc.com/

Calculators can be tedious tools on the computer, and Excel is sometimes too powerful for certain calculations. **Instacalc** calculates equations online as you type, and even does algebra for you. See their website for more examples, but its a great site to keep bookmarked.

Simple To-do list

http://workhack.com/

Some things don't need to be fancy to work, and a to-do list is one of them. For a simple, effective to-do list, use **WorkHack's Whiteboard**.

Argue Online

http://www.convinceme.net/

If you're the type of person who likes to argue, then you'll love taking part in online debates on **Convince Me**. It hosts four different types of debates: open, head to head, real-time, and king of the hill. It's interesting to see the opinions of other people, and is arguably better than arguing to the person's face.

Search for a Song by Humming

http://www.midomi.com/

If you've heard a song before, don't know the lyrics, but remember the general rhythm, you can hum the tune into your microphone and **Midomi** will tell you the name of the song.

Map Cell Phone Reception

http://www.cellreception.com/

Cell phone coverage is an issue to every cell phone subscriber at one point or another, so knowing where cell phone towers are in your neighborhood or in areas you're going to visit can help you get better reception. To see cell phone towers on a Google Map mashup, visit the above website.

Know Where to Run

http://www.walkjogrun.net/

Knowing how to run is one thing, but knowing where to run is another. A bad route can adversely affect your performance. Visiting the above website lets you search for routes other users have uploaded, plan your own route, calculate how many calories you'll burn, and upload your route for others to see. If you want to join a good running community, this is it.

Watch TV Shows, Cartoons, Movies, Documentaries, and More Online For Free

http://www.tv-links.co.uk/

To watch hundreds of TV shows, movies, and other videos online for free, visit **TV Links** at the above site. The site links to other sites that have the videos, and is a great way to watch the episodes of your favorite show you missed.

Use a Virtual Bookshelf to Show the Books You're Reading

http://www.shelfari.com/

If you love reading books and your friends do too, **Shelfari** makes it simple and fun to share the books you're reading with friends. You can discover new books to read, see what your friends and family are reading, and share your opinions of books.

Use Price Protection Policies

http://www.priceprotectr.com/

Many stores offer price protection policies that offer to refund the difference in price if the price of a purchased item goes down within 30 days of purchase. If you don't have time to keep track of the price, **Price Protectr** does the job for you. Give it the URL of the item and your email, and it will email you if the price go down. Apparently it has saved more than $250,000 for its users—good enough for me.

Downloads

Transfer Files Quickly and Easily Between Two Computers

http://www.tubesnow.com/

Getting files from one computer to the next can be a tedious process. If the computers are nearby, you can use an external drive to move the files, but the copying process may take time. If the computers are farther away, you can email the files, but most email providers set a limit to the amount of megabytes you can send per email. **Tubes** allows you to create a "tube" between the two computers, letting you send files from an application that is a similar to an instant messaging client. **Tubes** also allows you to sync files automatically, even when offline, so your most used files are up-to-date. Use **Tubes** to send files from work to home, school to home, between friends and family, and more.

See the Contents of Your Hard Drive

http://w3.win.tue.nl/nl/onderzoek/onderzoek_informatica/visualization/sequoiaview/

Finding out which programs or directories take up the most space on your hard drive can be difficult, so the free **SequoiaView** allows you to view a map of your hard drive, showing which files take up the most and least amount of space.

Get a Faster Acrobat Reader

http://www.foxitsoftware.com/pdf/rd_intro.php

The PDF file has become a common file format, but Acrobat Reader takes ages to load, something also attributed to Adobe Photoshop. A better alternative to Acrobat is **Foxit Reader**, which loads instantly and has the exact same functionality as Acrobat Reader. There is also an add-on you can buy that allows you to type and draw over the PDF so you can fill out a PDF electronically before printing it out.

Make Your Computer a Free Music and Video Server

http://www.orb.com/

Let's say you have a huge music collection on your computer and are going on vacation but do not want to (or cannot) take your computer with you. You could copy all the files to an external drive and then play them on another computer there, or you could use **Orb** to make your computer a music and video server so you can stream the music on any other computer, similar to an Internet radio station (though you pick the songs you want to play). If you have a TV tuner in your computer, you can also use Orb to stream live or recorded TV to another computer, so you can listen to your music or watch TV when away from home. Although you need a relatively large amount of computing power (see their System Requirements), most computers today fit the bill, and who can argue with the fact that it's free?

Put Your Computer in a Sandbox

http://www.sandboxie.com/

Many system actions, such as installing software or using Firefox, permanently change your hard drive. Rather than take a risk and uninstall potential viruses and malware, use **Sandboxie**. It allows you to do anything on your computer in a virtual sandbox, one that is between you and the hard drive. You can run Firefox in **Sandboxie**, so any malware downloaded is stuck in the sandbox and can be easily deleted by clearing **Sandboxie**. You can try software without having to change your system much, and unsolicited software gets wiped away when you clear the sandbox. **Sandboxie** is a better, free alternative to anti-virus tools, and is much more fool-proof.

Remove Obstructions from Photos

http://www.hanovsolutions.com/?prod=PhotoWipe

Consider this: you use your digital camera to take a photo on vacation and come home, only to realize that a perfect photo opportunity was ruined by some imperfection (someone else in the picture, for example). Simply use **Photowipe**, a free download, paint over the undesired object in black, and **Photowipe** will delete the obstruction, leaving only minor marks.

Load ISO Images Without Burning Discs

http://www.slysoft.com/en/virtual-clonedrive.html

Some software is too large to download, so programmers make them ISO images which need to be burned onto a disc to load; one example is if you want to install a Linux distribution, as almost all distributions demand that multiple CDs be burned. Rather than waste numerous discs, use **CloneDrive** to create a virtual drive, making the ISO image look like a CD even though it isn't and allowing the computer to open the ISO image.

The Google Earth NYC Expansion Pack

http://theori.st/nyc/index.html

New York City has so much to offer to tourists, but natives also need to find certain information from time to time, such as subway routes, police precinct locations, bike and parade routes, etc. The Google Earth Expansion Pack overlays New York City with the above information and more. All you have to do is go to My Places in Windows XP, create a new network link, and add "http://theori.st/nyc/nyc.kmz" (without the quotation marks) as the network link URL. This allows you to not only get the pack but also get updates by refreshing the link periodically. Alternatively, go to the website above for a direct download without the automatic updates option.

Identify Known Harmful Sites

http://www.trendsecure.com/portal/en-US/free_security_tools/trendprotect.php

Most Internet security tools take over your browser, asking you for permission to access every site. Rather, you can use **TrendProtect** to label each site as safe, unsafe, trusted, or unrated. Additionally, it will label the search results on Google, Yahoo, and MSN, so you can see what certain sites are rated before you visit them.

Change Certain Locked Functions of Windows

http://pitaschio.ara3.net/index.htm

Sometimes you just don't want the caps lock key to work, or maybe you want to adjust your volume with the mouse scroll wheel. If you want to change these, and more, functions of Windows, download **Pitaschio**. It allows you to adjust certain variables in Windows that would be harder to do without its easy-to-use interface.

Use Gmail as a Hard Drive

http://www.viksoe.dk/code/gmail.htm

http://gdisk.sourceforge.net/

Ever since Gmail started offering two gigabytes (and counting) of storage, your inbox could be surprisingly empty even if you had thousands of emails. But if you want to upload files, Gmail has a limit and takes a bit of time to upload your file. Therefore, you can use the **Gmail Drive Extension** for Windows and **gDisk** for Mac OS X. They create a literal drive in My Computer that allows you to drag and drop files and create folders just like a real drive. The files that you add appear in Gmail as an email, so you get the same functionality as uploading files to an email without the wait.

Automated Backups

http://www.nchsoftware.com/backup/index.html

If you want to backup your files automatically without having to bother doing it yourself, use **FileFort**. It allows you to select which files you want to backup and the frequency at which they're backed up—without you having to lay a finger on your computer once it boots up. Use an external drive, preferably one with 120 GB or more of storage, to back up your entire drive—just in case.

Block Out Part of Your Monitor When Watching a Video

http://teleskiving.wordpress.com/clutter-cloak/

Say you're watching a video on YouTube and want to watch the video without being distracted by the ads or other features on the page. Use the **Clutter Cloak Desktop Distraction Blocker** to gray out all the areas on the monitor except the area to which your mouse pointer is pointing.

Save Your Icons' Locations

http://www.dimanager.de/dimanager,en.html

In some cases, especially after you quit certain games that change your screen resolution, the locations of your icons may go back to their default positions on the left side of the desktop. If you organize your icons differently, reorganizing them repeatedly may be slightly annoying. Use the **DIManager X** desktop organizer, which allows you to create, save, and restore different desktop icon layouts.

Dim Your PC's Screen

http://www.whitsoftdev.com/powerdimmer/

Macs have the option of dimming the screen when not in use. To similarly dim the screen in Windows, use the **Power Dimmer Screensaver**. Simply extract the SCR (screensaver) file to the C:/Windows/system32/ folder, and select it as your default screensaver. You can change how long it takes for the screen to dim, as well as the final brightness level.

Rename Thousands of Files at Once

http://www.rlvision.com/flashren/about.asp

Anybody with a digital camera knows that the pictures don't have very descriptive names. Renaming all the files can take hours depending on how many pictures, or files in general, you have. The **Flash Renamer** allows you to change the case of the file names, replace strings of words in file names, and more. It allows you to organize your files quickly and easily, and you can use **Flash Renamer** with a fully-functional free trial.

See Your Inbox as a Beach Resort

http://www.3dmailbox.com/

If you have a few extra megabytes on your computer and want to see your emails as beachgoers taking in sun on the beach, download **3D Mailbox**. If a new email shows up, it has to get through the bouncer (the spam filter) and take a shower, and then swims in the pool until you read it, in which case it relaxes at the side of the pool. If you receive spam, it appears as a sumo wrestler. The program is a time-waster, but a very good one nevertheless.

Sign Your Emails With Your Latest Blog Post

http://www.blogsigs.com/

If you have a blog and want to tell your friends about it, check out **BlogSigs**. The freeware application signs your emails automatically with the name and link of your latest blog post.

Download YouTube Videos for Your PC and iPod

http://www.benjaminstrahs.com/

http://vconvert.net/

Use **Ares Tube** to download YouTube videos for viewing on your computer or transfer to your iPod. If you want to convert videos without downloading the **Ares Tube** program, use **Online FLV Converter**, the second site above.

Help Science With a Screensaver

http://folding.stanford.edu/

http://setiathome.berkeley.edu/

The **Folding@home** project was created by scientists
in order to understand protein folding. Since the
scientists don't have the computing power to run the
calculations they need, they offer a downloadable
program that runs as a screensaver but computes
calculations in the background. The results of the
calculations are sent back to the scientists, and the
results from all the computers are compiled. Other
projects are available, including one that searches for
extraterrestrial life (the second site listed above).
Because the calculations take such a toll on your CPU,
you should not initiate the screensaver when you're
doing work. If, however, you leave your computer for
a bit, the screensaver looks good, and you help
science: what else is better?

Save Paper Before You Print

http://www.printgreener.com/

When printing, especially off the Internet, some pages
will be virtually blank and have no real information
on them. **Greenprint**, a $35 program, makes it easy to
not print those pages with a few clicks. You'll save
money in the long run, and help the Earth as well.

Import Data from Graphs into Excel

http://digitizer.sourceforge.net/

If you have the picture of a graph and want to get the data from the graph into a spreadsheet, use **Engauge Digitizer**. Upload the image of the graph, select the data points, and **Engauge Digitizer** will give you a CSV file that you can open in Excel.

Understand Your Computer's Processes

http://www.processlibrary.com/processscan/

http://www.tasklist.org/

If you want to see what processes are happening behind the scenes of your computer, use **ProcessScanner**. Run the small download and it will upload all the processes to its server, give you a description of each one, and highlight those that may be harming your system's security. If **ProcessScanner** doesn't understand certain processes, check out **TaskList** and search for them manually.

Create Useful Shortcuts

http://programyaionela.republika.pl/english/tooler.htm

Use **Tooler,** a free download, to create shortcuts to shutdown your computer, set your volume to a particular setting, eject your CD tray, and more.

Create PDFs

http://www.dopdf.com/

It is often a difficult task to create PDFs, but **doPDF** makes it as easy as printing a document. When you see the document you wish to convert to a PDF, print it out, using the **doPDF** printer. Choose a name for the document and a location to save to, and you have a good quality PDF.

Draw on Your Screen

http://www.screenmarker.com/

In order to draw on your screen, for presentations or any number of other uses, use **Screen Marker**. You can pick any number of colors, and it's a great improvement over circling things with your mouse cursor alone.

Backup Your Files in Real-Time

http://www.mogware.com/filehamster/

If you want to create incremental backups of your work, freeware **FileHamster** is unprecedented. It doesn't interrupt your work flow, and creates a new backup of your files every time you save them. Although it was created for artists, its uses stem to just about every computer user.

Find Program Updates Automatically

http://www.filehippo.com/

Not updating your software often enough can mean security risks, decreased performance, and more, yet looking for the updates for each individual program can be tedious. Therefore, you can use **File Hippo Update Checker** to automatically tell you when there are updates available for your programs; it will even give you a direct link to the download.

Get Two or More PCs Networked Without a Wireless Router

http://www.wipeer.com/

If you want to communicate to another PC, but there is no WiFi router, Bluetooth, or other wireless signal available, **WiPeer** is an incredibly helpful tool. As long as all the computers have a wireless network card, **WiPeer** will create an Ad Hoc network that allows two or more PC users to chat, play multiplayer games, share files, and more.

Access PCs Remotely

http://www.crossloop.com/

http://www.tightvnc.com/

There are several remote access programs out there, but most demand that you to download a relatively large installation file and complete a tedious registration process that can lock you out of your PC if done incorrectly. Therefore, my choice for easy and secure remote computer access is **CrossLoop**. Both the host PC and the visiting PC download the same, two megabyte file. A 12 digit access code is created by the host computer, and entering that on the visiting PC will grant you access. Because you need permission every time you log in, the program is very secure but will not let you access the computer without another person on the other end granting you access; use VNC, LogMeIn, or GoToMyPC for one way remote access. Overall, this is the simplest and most intuitive remote access freeware I've encountered.

Free International Travel Guides

http://www.schmap.com/

If you travel to any major city for business or leisure, the freeware **Schmap Player** is a must. The downloadable player does not need Internet access to work, and features virtual tours, city search, trip planning, map, photo, and review integration, and more.

View Real-Time Traffic Cameras on Your Phone

http://www.freetrafficcam.com/

If you've ever been stuck in traffic, you know that getting traffic info, especially off your phone, is difficult. In New York, the **WCBS Video Cellmate** is an application that runs on many phones and allows you to view real-time traffic cameras.

Convert Google Gadgets and YouTube Videos into Windows Vista Gadgets

http://www.amnestywidgets.com/GeneratorWin.html

http://www.widgipedia.com/

Again, the title says it all. Use **Amnesty Generator** for Vista to convert the gadgets. Coupled with **Widgipedia**, which allows you to browse through widgets and gadgets from a number of providers, including Google Gadgets, Amnesty Generator can increase the number of gadgets available to you on Windows Vista.

Normalize the Volume of Your Mp3s

http://mp3gain.sourceforge.net/

If you have an iPod Shuffle or have mp3s that are from a variety of sources, you may end up reaching for the volume button for every track because some songs are too loud while others are too quiet. If you want to bring all the mp3s to the same volume, use **Mp3gain**. Its sole purpose is to normalize the volume on mp3s so you can listen to your music knowing you won't get startled by a track that is too loud.

Use Your Scanner and Printer as a Copier

http://icopy.sourceforge.net/

In its most basic form, a copier is a scanner and printer put together. Since that's the case, why do you need an actual copier when you can use your printer and scanner? The **iCopy** software links the two together, making it easy to scan the document, choose the number of copies you need, and print them right off your printer.

Take Your Office With You

http://portableapps.com/

If you want to take your programs with you wherever you go, buy a flash drive (256 megabytes or more, preferably 512 or more if you want to put other documents on it) and install the **PortableApps** program. It allows you to install and run the OpenOffice suite, Firefox, Thunderbird, Audacity, VLC Media Player, Gaim (an instant messaging client), 7-Zip, Mac OS 7, and other programs right off the drive. You can basically conduct your business off the drive so you leave nothing behind on other computers.

Buy a New Computer, Keep Your Old One

http://www.damnsmalllinux.org/

Buying a new computer with all the bells and whistles is a great experience, one that is so exhilarating you may feel your old computer is too "slow" to run anything. Before you put it on the curb, though, install the **Damn Small Linux** Linux distribution. This version of Linux is different because it has a very small installation file which the creators assure will never exceed fifty megabytes (small considering other Linux distributions can have installation files nearly three gigabytes in size). DSL also has very low minimum system requirements, so even the slowest of computers will be able to run it reasonably well. Check your email or browse the web quickly in the hallway or kitchen using the old computer, and leave your memory-intensive applications for the new one.

Linux has many applications that serve as free alternatives better than their commercial counterparts. For a decent list of Open Source alternatives for Windwos, Mac OS X, and Linux, visit **Osalt** at http://osalt.com/.

Try Ubuntu Linux Without the Potential for Messing Up Your Computer

http://www.wubi-installer.org/

Ubuntu Linux is one of the most popular Linux distributions, but it needs to partition your hard drive, and perhaps wipe out all of your data, as any other Linux distribution would. In order to circumvent this trouble, you can download **Wubi**, a free program that makes Ubuntu a simple program, easy to install, uninstall, and manage. You install **Wubi** like you would any other program without the need of burning CDs like you usually would for Linux, and you can try it out on your Windows PC for as long as you want with full access to all of Ubuntu's features. If you realize that you like Ubuntu more than Windows, you can go to Ubuntu's website, burn the required CDs, and install Ubuntu as the only operating system on your hard drive. On the other hand, if you realize that you don't like Ubuntu and want to continue with your version of Windows, just uninstall **Wubi**: no strings attached.

Free Your PC From Preinstalled Applications

http://www.pcdecrapifier.com/

Major PC manufacturers preinstall trial and full versions of software with new computers so they can lower the prices (and make more money off) of their computers. Manually uninstalling all the software may take hours, and some software is embedded into the computer, causing Windows to not allow you to uninstall them. **PC Decrapifier** finds all of the software on your compute, asks you which you want to uninstall, and then uninstalls them itself, letting you do other things on your computer.

Firefox Add-ons

Use Certain Websites Without Leaving a Trace

https://addons.mozilla.org/en-US/firefox/addon/1306

If there is a website you want to visit without leaving any evidence (history, cookies, downloaded files, saved form information, or otherwise) on the computer, use the **Stealther** add-on for Firefox. It allows you to activate and deactivate Firefox's privacy settings, so you can prevent your browser from remembering what you did without deleting your entire browsing history.

Open Multiple Links Quickly in Firefox

https://addons.mozilla.org/en-US/firefox/addon/4336

Rather than clicking links on a page individually, the Firefox add-on **Snap Links** allows you to draw a rectangle around the links (similar to highlighting multiple items on your desktop) and then open them in new tabs or windows.

Open Plain Text URLs in New Tabs

https://addons.mozilla.org/en-US/firefox/addon/4514

Sometimes URLs are not written as links on a web page, making it necessary to copy and paste the URL into a new tab or page if you want to open it. The **Smart Link** add-on for Firefox adds the "Open in New Tab" option to the right click menu, so you can highlight the URL, right-click it, and select "Open in New Tab" or "Open in New Window".

Separate Tabs by URL

https://addons.mozilla.org/en-US/firefox/addon/4913

When you open new tabs in Firefox, they are listed in the order in which they were opened, which is not very functional. Instead, download the **Separate Tabs** add-on for Firefox to list the tabs in groups by host URL (for example, all pages from Google would be listed together, all pages from Microsoft would be in another group, etc.).

Lock Firefox Passwords After Inactivity

https://addons.mozilla.org/en-US/firefox/addon/1275

Firefox's ability to save passwords for various sites is helpful, but it poses a security threat if anyone gains access to your computer. The Firefox add-on **Master Password Timeout** requires a master password to be entered after five minutes of inactivity before you can use your saved passwords.

Find Your Way Back in Firefox

https://www.squarefree.com/extensions/high/

Many Internet sites lead you from one page to another, so you have to repeatedly hit "Back" to get to the source page. The **How'd I Get Here?** add-on for Firefox allows you to click one button to go back to a search results page after you've looked at one of the results and view the origin of a bookmark you added previously, among other uses.

Search Any Site from Firefox's Built-In Search Bar

https://addons.mozilla.org/en-US/firefox/addon/3682

If you search sites other than the ones available in Firefox's search bar frequently, the **Add to Search Bar** Firefox add-on allows you to right-click on the search box of any website and add that search to the built-in Firefox search bar (located at the top right corner of the window) so you don't have to navigate to the page to search it.

Find Coupons Available for a Website Quickly and Easily

https://addons.mozilla.org/en-US/firefox/addon/5408

There are always coupons available for websites, and saving a few bucks here and there never hurt. Install the **Coupon Craze Coupon Notifier** add-on for Mozilla Firefox. It lists some available coupons for the site you are currently visiting.

Miscellany

Reduce the Size of Powerpoint Presentations

http://www.scribd.com/

http://www.slideshare.net/

Powerpoint presentations are used constantly in schools and businesses, but transporting the files can be tedious since they can be extraneously large. Most large files are caused by various forms of media, particularly images. To reduce the size of Powerpoint files, do the following:

1. If the pictures you copied are BMP or TIFF files, open them in Microsoft Paint and save them as JPEG files. JPEG files are smaller and are similar in quality.

2. Try compressing the pictures by right-clicking them and selecting the "Format Picture" option. Select the option with the lowest PPI setting (usually the the Web Setting).

If the file is still too large, try uploading it to Scribd or Slideshare, websites that allow you to download the original Powerpoint from anywhere you have Internet access or view it as a Flash video.

Shut Off Peripherals Automatically

http://www.smarthomeusa.com/Shop/Hardware-Cable/Item/LCG1/

Computer peripherals use power when idle, and coupled with the addition of more peripherals is less initiative to shut each individual gadget off. Therefore, the **Smart Strip Power Strip** senses when you shut your computer off, and then shuts off your computer's peripherals so you don't have to. It doubles as a surge protector, so you protect your investments and save money and the environment.

Faster Data Entry

If you have to enter a lot of data into a file (a spreadsheet, for example), try reading the data and recording it in any audio recorder (Audacity, for example), and then playing it back while entering it into the document. It is similar to having another person read you the data, and is certainly faster than glancing back and forth between your monitor and the information source.

Make MP3s Act Like Audiobooks in iTunes

Audiobooks remember where you leave off when you go to a new song so you can continue from that point the next time you listen to it. The same functionality can be extended to any mp3 with a small change: simply go to the Options tab in the Get Info menu of iTunes and check the "Remember Playback Position" box, thus causing your mp3s to act like audiobooks with the additional functionality. You have to check each song individually, so to save time you can apply it only to the longer songs and leave the shorter ones unchanged.

Watch Videos from Your iPod on Your TV Cheaply

Apple charges $99 for its AV connection kit, which allows you to watch videos from your iPod on TV. But you can get an A/V to RCA cable from RadioShack for as little as $20, and even half that on eBay. The difference? Apple switched a few colors around on the wires, so plugging an A/V to RCA cable into your iPod while following the colors on the cable won't work. But if you plug the red RCA cable into your TV's yellow jack, the yellow RCA cable into your TV's white jack, and the white RCA cable into the TV's red jack, set your iPod Video's TV Out Option to Yes, and plug in the 3.5 mm plug into your iPod, you should get video on your TV.

View Webcams From All Over the World

Many people who own webcams make them accessible from the Web—and don't secure them. With a simple Google search, you can view webcams showing everything from parks and sidewalks to, well, just search. Enter the following search strings to view most of the unsecured webcams on the Net. Some webcams even let you look around, tilt the camera, and zoom in and out. You can also visit http://www.opentopia.com/hiddencam.php to browse webcams by country, although you'll get a bigger selection by searching the following on Google:

inurl:"MultiCameraFrame?Mode="

inurl:"ViewerFrame?Mode="

inurl:"view/index.shtml"

inurl:"axis-cgi/mjpg"

Microsoft's TiVo

http://www.dragonglobal.org/showanalyzer.html

http://babgvant.com/files/folders/dvrmstoolbox/entry5169.aspx

http://www.scendix.com/mceauction/

http://www.embeddedautomation.com/EAHAmControl.htm

Most people don't know that Microsoft offers an alternative to TiVo that's actually compelling to use. The product? Vista Premium or Ultimate Edition. How so? Well, those versions of Vista come built in with Media Center, allowing you to control music, photos, videos, and TV—right off your computer. A great setup would include a small (but powerful—dual core, 2 GB RAM) machine connected to both a monitor and a TV. By doing so, you can record and watch TV and tools such as **ShowAnalyzer** and **DVRSToolbox** that remove commercials from TV shows and let you convert the recorded material and **MceAuction**, which allows you to bid on auctions on eBay and alerts you if you were outbid on an auction while you're watching TV, all for free. Additionally, you can buy **mControl** for $75 to automate your lighting and security systems, and control everything from your PC. And you needed another reason to upgrade to Vista?

Run Mac OS X on a PC

http://wiki.osx86project.org/wiki/index.php/Main_Page

When I said earlier that Mac OS X doesn't run on any computer but those made by Apple, I lied. Well, it wasn't really a lie, considering it's highly illegal, difficult, and overall pointless. If you have the heart and patience to go about doing it, though, visit the above website. It gives directions you can follow to get Mac OS X to run on your PC. Basically you create a backup of your Mac's drive on your PC's drive, making the PC's drive look like an external hard drive (Apple allows you to make one backup of your Mac's drive legally) and then placing the drive back into your PC. Remember, the standard disclaimer rules (available on pages 149 and 150) apply.

Do-It-Yourself Headphones Holder

Headphones can end up in a tangled mess, but here are few solutions on the market that keep headphones untangled. To create a free headphone holder that keeps your headphones neatly wrapped, cut a credit card in half lengthwise. Next, cut a small notch in the upper part of one of the halves so the it ends up looking like the figure above. To wrap your headphones, place the earpieces inside of the notch,

then wrap the cord around the card.

Hidden Game in OpenOffice Calc

Open source companies are often more down-to-earth than their commercial counterparts, and this hidden feature displays just that. Start OpenOffice Calc (Excel's parallel) and type the following into the first cell of the spreadsheet exactly how it appears without a period at the end: =Game("StarWars"). This will launch a hidden but built-in "Star Wars" game that is just right for the times when you've had enough of solitaire and minesweeper.

Google Earth Flight Simulator

http://earth.google.com/intl/en/userguide/v4/flightsim/index.html

Google Earth is an amazing program to use for fun, and the addition of a hidden flight simulator in the latest version of Google Earth simply reduces any resistance you might have had to downloading it. The flight simulator allows you to fly one of two planes taking off from one of several airports, such as New York's JFK and London's Heathrow. You can also fly a plane from a current view, so you can fly right above your house. To launch the simulator, press and hold the control and alternate (abbreviated as "ctrl" and "alt" on most keyboards, respectively), and then press the "A" key (on Macs, press and hold the command and option buttons, abbreviated as "cmd" and "opt", and then press the "A" key). Visit the above website to learn the controls involved.

Google Tips

Search for Only Faces in Google

If you want to search for a human who shares a name with a place or thing (Paris, for example), add the string "&imgtype=face" (without the quotation marks) to the end of the URL of any image search. Google will then restrict the search results to pictures of people.

Search for an Exact Phrase

Let's say you want to search for a restaurant named "Surf Water" on Google. Without the quotation marks, Google will search for the two words separately, so you'll get a lot of surfing websites and not the website of the restaurant. In cases like this, it is sometimes better to search the term with quotation marks around it, in which case Google will search for the explicit phrase.

Either...Or

If you want to search for either one term or another, use the OR operator (the OR must be capitalized). For example, if you want to search for either the term "Acer" or "Sony", search: Acer OR Sony.

Search for a Range of Numbers

If you want to find results for a range of numbers, use Google's numeric range operator (two periods between the two numbers). For example, if you want to search for the presidents in office from 1970 to 2000, search: president 1970..2000

Google as a Calculator

To calculate relatively simple equations quickly, type the equation into Google and search for it. For example, searching "4*3" will give you the result 12.

Google as a Dictionary

If you want to find the definition of a word, type "define:", followed by the word, into Google. For example, to find the definition of the word "coagulate", search the following: define: coagulate.

Find a Telephone Number with Google Phone Book

Since the Yellow Pages went online, it was only a matter of time until Google indexed the site. Yet Google went one step further and added phone numbers to their home page, so if you type in a telephone number, you should get the name of the associated person or business (unless they removed their name—see next entry).

Remove Your Phone Number from the Google Phone Book

http://www.google.com/help/pbremoval.html

Google has a helpful feature that allows you to search for a telephone number and get the name associated with the telephone number. If you yourself do not want your number and name to appear, you can remove your information at the above address. Keep in mind, though, that once your number is removed it can never be added again.

Use Google for Conversions

To convert anything to anything else (with reason) just type it into Google. For example, 4 cups in teaspoons, 4.9 gigabytes in kilobytes, 10 euros in dollars, etc.

Search Only One Domain

If you want to run a search on one domain without searching the whole Internet, use Google's domain operator. For example, if you want to search for Parliament on the BBC News site, search on Google: parliament site:www.bbc.co.uk

Search for a Certain File Type

If you're looking for a file with a specific file format, add the term "filetype:" and the file type you want. For example, if you want a PDF file about computers, search: "computer" filetype:pdf

Exclude Domains from a Search

Sometimes you want to search for a term without having certain sites searched. Therefore, use the exclude domain operator. For example, to search for Wikipedia on all sites except wikipedia.org, enter : wikipedia -site:wikipedia.org

Find a Song's Name by Using its Lyrics

If you hear a few words from a song but do not know the name of the song, search for: lyrics: examplehere, replacing "examplehere" with the lyrics you heard. Google will then return sites that contain the remaining lyrics, the song's name, and artist.

Find Toll-Free Customer Service Numbers

If you want to find the customer service numbers on a website but do not want to dig through the entire site to find them, type the name of the company followed by 800 OR 877 OR 866 OR 888. For example, to find Circuit City's customer service number, type: circuit city 800 OR 877 OR 866 OR 888.

Get the Local Date and Time in Any City

If you want to find the date and time in any city but do not want to actually convert the time yourself, type the word time followed by the name of the city in quotation marks. For example: time "London"

Download Free Comic Books

Comic books are often stored in the CBR or CBZ format. By searching on Google for the following searches and renaming the file with the ZIP extension (.zip) for CBZ files or the RAR extension (.rar) for CBR files and then using 7-Zip to unpack both, you can read comic books using Cdisplay on Windows or FFView on Mac OS X. To search for comics with the CBR and CBZ formats (respectively), search for the following:

-inurl:htm -inurl:html intitle:"index of" "Last modified" comics cbr

-inurl:htm -inurl:html intitle:"index of" "Last modified" comics cbz

To search for the comics that are stored in the RAR or ZIP format to begin with, replace the "cbr" and "cbz" above with "rar" and "zip" respectively. To search for a specific comic, replace "comics" above with the name of the comic.

Browse Catalogs

http://catalogs.google.com/

Browse hundreds of catalogs in a number of categories by visiting Google Catalogs. Although you cannot buy directly from the catalog, you can call up the vendor and order from them. It saves time and paper, and leaves your mailbox free of clutter.

View a Website Even When It Doesn't Work

Sometimes websites don't load because of a problem with the site (not a problem with your Internet connection). To view the website anyway, search for the site in Google, and then click the "cached" option that appears in blue below the search listing. Google caches its listings often, so you'll get a relatively recent version of the site.

Subtract Words from a Google Search

If you're searching for something that applies to two categories, Google won't know which category it applies to. Therefore, Google allows you to subtract words from your search by using a minus sign. For example, if you search for virus, you may be thinking of a virus that affects humans, not computers. You could then search: virus -computer.

Other Google Services

Google Translate

http://www.google.com/language_tools?hl=en

Google offers a translating service for words, phrases, and sentences between a number of languages, including English, Spanish, French, Chinese, Korean, Portuguese, Arabic, and more. Google also understands the different meanings words in various languages have, so it gives you different translation options based on the context.

Google News

http://news.google.com/

Google News offers news stories from a variety of sources and countries discussing various topics. It is a great way to get a complete palette of stories quickly.

Gmail

http://gmail.com

Gmail is one of the leading competitors in the web mail market and is my favorite. Its clean look is complimentary to the Google homepage, and its two gigabyte (and growing) capacity is more than enough for most users. The integrated search scans through your messages, so looking for that email from last week or month is as easy as completing a Google web search. It also has integrated Google Talk functionality, so if a friend or family member is logged into Gmail when you are, you can send instant messages to them.

Google Video and YouTube

http://video.google.com/

http://www.youtube.com/

Google Video was Google's primary video search until

it bought YouTube; to most people today, the distinction between the two is nonexistent. However, Google Video is now an overarching video search that searches several video services, including YouTube, whereas YouTube is a video service unto its own.

Google Product Search and Google Checkout

http://www.google.com/prdhp?

http://checkout.google.com/

Google Product Search, formerly Froogle, makes finding the products you're looking for easy to find. Items are sorted by price, retailer, and more. Once you find the product you want, some retailers allow you to pay with Google Checkout, an easier, safer alternative to Paypal.

iGoogle

http://www.google.com/ig?

iGoogle, formerly Google Personalized Homepage, is a page you can customize with your own gadgets, convenient for having all your information in one central location (making it good for a homepage). Users can choose what gadgets they wish to include, the organization of said gadgets, and options pertaining to each individual gadget.

Google Docs and Spreadsheets

http://docs.google.com/

Google's purchase of the Internet start-up Writely launched it into the web document business. It allows users to create and edit word and spreadsheet documents online. The primary advantage is to make the process of sharing documents quick and easy, and it also allows you to access your documents from anywhere you have Internet access.

Google Finance

http://finance.google.com/

Use Google Finance as a stock ticker. It's price history and news feeds make it a great way to research potential investments.

Google Pack

http://pack.google.com/

Google Pack allows you to download Google products and services together, with the ability to update the programs automatically with the included Google update software.

Google Notebook

http://google.com/notebook/

This Google service allows you to compile information from the web in a document online without tedious copying and pasting.

Google Earth

http://earth.google.com/

Google Earth is Google's satellite imagery program, providing high quality aerial photos of the entire world. Most of its users run the program for leisure, but some news agencies use the software for demonstration purposes.

Picasa

http://picasa.google.com/

Picasa is a handy photo editing tool that makes digital photos look great. The user interface is easy to use, and the software makes dark photos lighter, eliminates red eyes, improves the contrast ratio, and more.

Google Web Accelerator

http://webaccelerator.google.com/

Broadband connections may be fast, but additional performance is always welcome. Google Web Accelerator caches your data, shaving a few seconds off the loading time of each website. Note that although Google says it does not cache data from secure websites for security reasons, you may not want to install this software if you handle very important, secure files and websites, even if Google promises to look the other way.

Google Desktop

http://desktop.google.com/

Google Desktop is a Vista sidebar-like software download that allows you to quickly search for files on your computer. Again, Google caches the data, so don't use this software if you have confidential files. If you don't, though, Google's search for your computer is as easy to use as its web search. Google's gadget collection has thousands of submissions, so you can personalize your sidebar as much as you like.

Google 411

http://labs.google.com/goog411/

Google's telephone map search option, currently in beta testing, allows you to call a number, say a city and state or type in the zip code, and say or type the business name or category, and will then give you the top search results. It will automatically connect you to the business you choose, and you can also ask to be sent a text message with details of one of the search results and the link to a map of the business. It's a very useful tool to have on the road when you do not have access to a map or Google.

Part 3

How-to and Troubleshooting

Microsoft Windows

To start your computer:

1. Look for a button that looks like the one to the right, or one that says power or on/off.

2. Press it.

To log into your computer:

1. If you don't have a password and have one account on the computer, the computer will usually log in automatically.

2. If you don't have a password but have multiple accounts on the computer, you will have to select an account to log into. Press the picture or name of one of the accounts to log into that account.

3. If you have one or more accounts that are password protected, you will have to click on the account and enter the password by typing it on the keyboard. The password will appear as small black dots for privacy reasons.

To change your desktop picture:

1. Right click on your desktop.

2. In the resulting menu, click "Properties".

3. In the resulting menu, click on the tab towards the top of the windows that says "Desktop".

4. Choose the picture you want by clicking once on each of the names of the various pictures and looking at the preview that should show on a small computer screen in the same window. To scroll through the list, click on the arrows that point up and down on the side of the list of names. By clicking the "Browse" button, you can select a picture on your computer to use as a desktop background.

5. Click "Apply".

6. Click "OK".

To change your screensaver:

1. Right click on your desktop.

2. In the resulting menu, click "Properties".

3. In the resulting menu, click on the tab towards the top of the window that says "Screensaver".

4. Choose the screensaver you want by clicking once on each of the names of the various

screensavers and looking at the preview that should show on a small computer screen in the same window. To scroll through the list, click on the arrows that point up and down on the side of the list of names.

5. Click "Apply".

6. Click "OK".

To turn off your computer:

1. Click "Start".

2. Click "Turn Off Computer".

3. In the resulting menu, click "Turn Off".

To restart your computer:

1. Click "Start".

2. Click "Turn Off Computer".

3. In the resulting menu, click "Restart".

To put your computer to sleep:

1. Click "Start".

2. Click "Turn Off Computer".

3. In the resulting menu, click "Standby".

To add a printer to your computer:

1. Connect the printer cable to the computer.

2. Turn the printer on.

3. If you have a CD with the printer driver, put it into your CD tray. If the CD automatically loads, follow the on-screen instructions. If not, click "Start", then "My Computer", then double click your CD drive, then double click on the installation file. If you downloaded the driver from online, run the file by double clicking the installation file. If there is no installation file, simply note the location of other printer files.

4. Click "Start".

5. Click "Printers and Faxes".

6. In the right-hand panel in the resulting panel, click "Add a Printer".

7. Follow the on-screen instructions, telling the computer where the installation files are.

Adjust your system's volume:

1. In the right hand corner of the screen in the taskbar, click once on a speaker-like icon.

2. Drag the bar in the resulting menu up to increase volume and down to decrease volume.

Create or Change Your Windows password:

1. Click "Start".

2. Click "Control Panel".

3. If the left-hand panel contains the words "Switch to Category View", then do not do anything. If the words "Switch to Classic View" are there, click them.

4. Double click on the "User Accounts" button.

5. Click the "Change an Account" link.

6. Click on the account that has the password you wish to change.

7. If you do not already have a password, click the "Create a Password" link and type in your desired password, following the on-screen instructions. If you already have a password and wish to change it, click the "Change My Password" link. Type in your old password and your new password, and click the "Change Password" button. You can also add a password hint, one that is available to everyone who encounters the Windows log-in screen. The hint should not reveal your password, but should help you remember it.

Automatically backup your files:

1. Launch Mozilla Firefox.

2. Visit the following site:
   http://www.nchsoftware.com/backup/index.html

3. Download the "FileFort" program.

4. Select which files you want to backup, as well as the frequency at which they will be backed up. The program allows all files in the selected folders to be backed up, only the files that were changed since the last backup to be backed up, or only the files changed in the previous 24 hours to be backed up. Follow the on-screen directions and backup to an external drive.

Openoffice Writer

Openoffice writer is similar to Microsoft Word, so learning the basics of Openoffice programs will help you in other word processing programs.

To start Openoffice Writer:

1. Click on Start.

2. Click on All Programs.

3. In the resulting menu, click on the folder labeled "OpenOffice".

4. In the resulting menu, click on the file named "OpenOffice Writer".

5. To begin writing a document, simply start typing.

To highlight and select certain text:

1. Place the cursor to the immediate left of the first character of the text you want to select.

2. Click the left mouse button, and at the same time drag the cursor to the immediate right of the last character of the text you want to select.

To highlight and select the entire document:

Either

1. On the top menu bar (where the selections include "File", "Edit", "View", "Insert", etc.), click on "Edit".

2. In the resulting menu, click "Select All".

Or

1. While pressing and holding the control key (abbreviated as "ctrl") on the keyboard, press the letter "A".

To cut selected text (removing it and placing it on the clipboard until pasting):

Either

1. On the top menu bar (where the selections include "File", "Edit", "View", "Insert", etc.), click on "Edit".

2. In the resulting menu, click "Cut".

Or

1. While pressing and holding the control key (abbreviated as "ctrl") on the keyboard, press the letter "X".

To copy selected text (keeping its location but placing it on the clipboard as well until pasting):

Either

1. On the top menu bar (where the selections include "File", "Edit", "View", "Insert", etc.), click on "Edit".

2. In the resulting menu, click "Copy".

Or

1. While pressing and holding the control key (abbreviated as "ctrl") on the keyboard, press the letter "C".

To paste previously copied or cut text:

1. On the top menu bar (where the selections include "File", "Edit", "View", "Insert", etc.), click on "Edit".

2. In the resulting menu, click "Paste".

Or

1. While pressing and holding the control key (abbreviated as "ctrl") on the keyboard, press the letter "V".

To change the font of selected text:

1. Follow the above directions to select text.

2. Click on the triangle in the drop-down box in the top menu bar that should say by default "Times New Roman", but may list other font names.

3. Scroll up and down in the remaining menu by clicking on the up and down arrows on the side

of the menu until you find the font you want.

4. Click on the name of the font you want.

To change the size of selected text:

1. Follow the above directions to select text.

2. Click in the triangle in the drop-down box in the top menu bar that should say by default "14", but may list other font sizes.

3. Scroll up and down in the remaining menu by clicking on the up and down arrows on the side of the menu until you find the font size you want.

4. Click on the font size you want.

To make selected text bold:

1. Follow the above directions to select text.

2. Press and hold the control button (abbreviated as "ctrl" on the keyboard) and then press the "B" key.

To make selected text italicized:

1. Follow the above directions to select text.

2. Press and hold the control button (abbreviated

as "ctrl" on the keyboard) and then press the "I" key.

To make selected text underlined:

1. Follow the above directions to select text.
2. Press and hold the control button (abbreviated as "ctrl" on the keyboard) and then press the "U" key.

To launch spellcheck:

Either

1. In the top menu bar, click on "Tools".
2. In the resulting menu, click on "Spellcheck".

Or

1. Press the "F7" key on the keyboard.

To save a document for the first time:

1. In the top menu bar, click on "File".
2. In the resulting menu, click on "Save As".
3. If you want to save the document on the desktop, click "Desktop" on the left side of the resulting menu. If you want to save in "My

Documents", click "My Documents" in the resulting menu. If you want to save in another location, click on the triangle in the drop-down menu that appears next to the words "Save in:".

4. Type a name for the document in the textbox next to the words "File Name:".

5. Click the "Save" button that appears next to the textbox mentioned in step 4.

To save a document for the second and successive times:

Either

1. In the top menu bar, click on "File".

2. In the resulting menu, click on "Save".

Or

1. While pressing and holding the control key (abbreviated as "ctrl" on the keyboard), click on the "S" key.

To save a document in the Microsoft Word 97/2000/XP format in order to open the file in Microsoft Word:

1. In the top menu bar, click on "File".

2. In the resulting menu, click on "Save As".

3. Select the file saving location and the file name.

4. Click on the triangle in the drop-down menu that appears next to the words "Save as type:"

5. In the resulting menu, click on the "Microsoft Word 97/2000/XP (.doc)" option.

6. Click the "Save" button.

To save the document as a PDF file:

1. In the top menu bar, click "File".

2. In the resulting menu, click on "Export as PDF".

3. In the resulting menu, select a file saving location and a file name.

4. Click "Save".

5. In the resulting menu, press the "Export" button that appears towards the bottom of the window.

To print a document:

1. In the top menu bar, click "File".

2. In the resulting menu, click on "Print".

3. In the resulting menu, select the printer you will use by clicking on the triangle on the drop-down menu that appears next to the word "Printer:".

4. Select the number of copies of the document you want, by default set at 1, by selecting the "1" in the textbox that appears next to the words "Number of copies:" and typing in the number of copies you want.

5. Select which pages of the document you want to print, by default set to print all pages, by clicking on the button that appears to the left of the word "Pages:", selecting the number that appears in the textbox to the right of the word "Pages:" and typing in the pages you want to print. For example, if you want to print the pages 1 through 10, type "1-10". If you want to print pages 1, 4, and 9 through 11, type "1, 4, 9-11", and so on.

6. Click the "OK" button.

To insert a table into the document:

Either

1. Click "Table" in the top menu bar.

2. In the resulting menu, click "Insert".

3. In the resulting menu, click "Table".

Or

1. Press and hold the control key (abbreviated as

"ctrl" on the computer keyboard) and then press the "F12" key.

Then

1. Select the number of columns your table will have, by default, 2, by selecting the number that appears in the textbox next to the word "Columns:".

2. Select the number of rows your table will have, by default, 2, by selecting the number that appears in the textbox next to the word "Rows:".

3. Click "OK".

To insert columns or rows into a table:

1. Create a table.

2. Click in a cell to the left or right of where you want a column to go or above or below where you want a row to go.

3. In the top menu bar, click "Table".

4. In the resulting menu, click "Insert".

5. In the resulting menu, click either "Rows" or "Columns".

6. In the resulting menu, change the number of rows or columns you will add, by default 1, by

selecting the number that appears in the textbox next to the word "Amount" and typing the desired number.

7. If you placed the cursor to the left or above where you want a column or row to go, click on the button "Before" that appears below the heading "Position". If you placed the cursor to the right or below where you want a column or row to go, click on the button "After" that appears below the heading "Position".

8. Click "OK".

To search for a word in the document, and optionally replace words:

Either

1. Click on "Edit" in the top menu bar.

2. In the resulting menu, click "Find & Replace".

Or

1. Press and hold the control key (abbreviated as "ctrl" on the keyboard), and then press the "F" key.

Then

1. In the textbox under the words "Search for", type the word you are looking for.

2. To optionally replace the word you look for with another word, type the replacement word in the textbox under the words "Replace with".

3. To highlight the word(s) you were looking for one at a time, click on the "Find" button.

4. To highlight the word(s) you were looking for altogether, click in the "Find All" button.

Mozilla Firefox

To install Firefox:

1. Open Internet Explorer by clicking on Start, then "All Programs", and then the icon that says "Internet Explorer".

2. Once Internet Explorer starts, go to the URL bar and type in the following link: http://www.google.com/

3. When the Google page appears, type the word "Firefox" into the search bar and press the "Enter" key.

4. Click on the first link on the resulting page.

5. Click the "Download" button on the resulting page.

6. When Internet Explorer asks you whether to run or save the file, click "Run".

7. Follow the on-screen instructions to install Firefox.

To launch Firefox:

Either

1. Click on "Start".

2. In the resulting menu, click on "All Programs".

3. In the resulting menu, click on the "Mozilla Firefox" folder.

4. In the resulting menu, click "Mozilla Firefox".

5. If Firefox asks you if it should be the default browser, click "Yes".

Or

1. Double click on the "Mozilla Firefox" icon on your desktop.

2. If Firefox asks you if it should be the default browser, click "Yes".

To visit a website:

1. Double click on the URL bar towards the top of the window.

2. Type in the name of the website you want to visit.

   3. Press the "Enter" button.

To go back a page:

1. Click on the arrow facing left in the bar towards the top of the window.

To go forward a page:

1. Click on the arrow facing right in the bar towards the top of the window.

To bookmark a website:

1. Go to a website.
2. Click on the "Bookmarks" menu that appears in the menu bar at the top of the window.
3. In the resulting menu, click "Bookmark This Page". Alternatively you press and hold the Control key (abbreviated as "ctrl" on the keyboard) and then press the "D" key.
4. Type a name for the bookmark (usually the given one is sufficient).
5. Press the "OK" button.

To clear the cookies, history, and other information from Mozilla Firefox:

1. Launch Mozilla Firefox.

2. Click the Tools menu that appears in the menu bar towards the top of the window.

3. In the resulting menu, click on the "Clear Private Data" option. Alternatively, you can press the control, shift, and delete keys on your keyboard (control may be abbreviated as "ctrl" and delete may be abbreviated as "del").

4. Check all the options you want to delete, and uncheck all the ones you don't want to delete. To understand what each option means, refer to the following:

   1. Browsing history: Deleting this will delete the list of all the sites you've visited. Deleting the list probably won't result in a significant gain in your computer's performance, but you may want to delete for privacy reasons.

   2. Downloading history: Deleting this will delete the list within Firefox of all the files you've downloaded. Keep in mind the the actual files will still be on your computer unless you delete them separately. Again, no performance gain will result as privacy is the main concern.

3. Saved form and search history: Firefox has the option of saving the information you write in online forms so you don't have to enter it repeatedly. Additionally, Firefox saves your search history so you can access frequently searched terms quickly and easily. If you don't want this information to appear in Firefox, delete this information. Still no performance gain will result from deleting this information.

4. Cache: The cache is very similar to the RAM on your computer, and lets you view frequently visited pages faster by saving the page and other information. Deleting this will make your browsing experience a bit slower, but you may want to delete it every once in a while since it can be retrieved. Additionally, having a cache does have a trade-off— specifically that Firefox has to decide whether to load pages from the Internet or from the cache, resulting in pages that are outdated. To counter this problem, refresh pages that depend on frequent updating, such as blogs.

5. Cookies: Cookies are small files that websites leave on your computer to access the next time you visit the website. Cookies can be both helpful and harmful, so clearing them often will actually speed up your computer a

bit (and free up some space).

6. Saved passwords: Firefox gives you the option to save the passwords to websites so you don't have to repeatedly enter them. You can clear them for privacy reasons, though it won't affect system performance.

Gmail

To create a Gmail account:

1. Double click on the URL bar towards the top of the page.

2. Type in "www.google.com".

3. On the resulting page, type "Gmail" into the search box.

4. Press the "Enter" key.

5. Click on the first link on the resulting page.

6. Click on the "Sign Up" link.

7. Follow the on-screen instructions. Some fields with which you may need help:

    1. Desired login name: type in the email you want (for example, if you want the email "exampleemail@gmail.com", type "exampleemail" in the desired login name box.

2. Choose a password: type in the password you want to access your email with. Refer to page 18 for tips on good password security. Google requires you to type in your password twice to ensure that they match; if they don't, a new page will load and you'll have to reenter your password.

3. Security question: Choose a question from the list or click on "Write my own question" to specify a question of your own. If you ever forget your password, Google will ask you the question and providing the correct answer will allow you to reset your password.

8. Press the "I accept. Create my account." button towards the bottom of the page after you read the Terms and Conditions.

To log into your Gmail account:

1. Launch Mozilla Firefox.

2. Double click on the URL bar towards the top of the window.

3. Type "www.google.com".

4. Press the "Enter" key.

5. Type "Gmail" in the resulting page.

6. Press the "Enter" key.

7. Press on the first link on the resulting page; it should say "Welcome to Gmail".

8. On the right hand side of the resulting page, enter your email in the textbox labeled "Username" and your password in the textbox labeled "Password". For example, if your email address is "exampleemail@gmail.com" and your password is "testpassword1", type "exampleemail" into the textbox labeled "Username" and "testpassword1" into the textbox labeled "Password".

9. Press the "Enter" key.

10. Additionally, if you want to bookmark the Gmail page so you can access it quickly, refer to page 123.

To view your new mail in Gmail:

1. Log into your Gmail account.

2. Your unread mail will be on the resulting page.

To read an email in Gmail:

1. Log into your Gmail account.

2. Click on one of the emails that appear in the

inbox (or in the "All Mail" list; read on for more information).

To write an email in Gmail:

1. Log into your Gmail account.

2. Click on the "Compose mail" link located towards the top left side of the resulting page.

3. Click on the textbox to the left of the word "To:".

4. Type the recipient's email address. If there is more than one recipient, separate the emails with commas just as you would items in a list.

5. Click on the textbox to the left of the word "Subject:".

6. Type the subject of your email. This will be what the recipient sees before he/she opens the email. If you do not want to write a subject, do not type anything, but keep in mind that the recipient may not want to open the email without a given subject.

7. Click on the big white box that appears two rows or so below the subject textbox.

8. Type your email. To certain words of your email bold, italicized, or underlined, highlight and click on the corresponding "B", "I", and "U" that appear above the body of the email, just as

you would in OpenOffice.

9. To check the spelling of the email, click on the "Check Spelling" link that appears towards the right side of the window.

10. When you are sure you wrote everything correctly, send the email by clicking the "Send" button that appears towards the top of the window. You can alternatively save the email or throw it out by clicking on the corresponding buttons that appear next to the "Send" button.

To archive an email in Gmail:

One of Gmail's main features is the ability to archive emails, meaning they'll be stored away, available to be searched or browsed but not viewed in the normal inbox folder. To archive an email:

1. Select one or more emails in the inbox by clicking on the check box(es) that appears below the word "Select" and to the left of the email.

2. Click on the "Archive" button that appears towards the top of the window and to the left of the "Report Spam" button.

To search emails in Gmail:

1. Click on the textbox that appears to the right of

the Gmail logo towards the top of the window.

2. Type the desired search term.

3. Click the "Search Mail" button that appears to the right of the textbox.

4. The resulting page will list all the emails in which the search term exists. Keep in mind this will search both archived emails and those in your inbox.

To browse all emails:

1. Click on the "All Mail" link that appears towards the left of the window directly above the "Spam" link.

To report an email as spam:

1. Select one or more emails in the inbox by clicking on the check box(es) that appears below the word "Select" and to the left of the email.

2. Click the "Report Spam" button that appears towards the top of the window.

Miscellany

To visit Google:

1. Launch Mozilla Firefox.
2. In the URL bar, type "www.google.com".
3. Press the "Enter" key.

To create a free website:

1. Launch Mozilla Firefox.
2. Visit Google.
3. Search for "Google Pages".
4. Click on the first link.
5. Enter your Gmail username and password in the resulting page.
6. Click on the "Create a new page" link.
7. Type a name for the new page, then click the "Create and Edit" button.
8. The resulting page has a fairly user friendly interface, making it easy to create a free website. Follow the on-screen instructions.

To create a free blog:

A blog is an online journal, enabling you to share your

experiences and thoughts with others.

1. Launch Mozilla Firefox.

2. Visit Google.

3. Search for "Blogger".

4. Press the "Enter" key.

5. Enter your Gmail username and password in the resulting page.

6. Follow the on-screen instructions.

To get Internet access at Starbucks, various hotels, and any paid wireless Internet in a public environment, for free:

Many establishments today offer paid high speed wireless Internet access, although the prices are often outrageously out-of-line. There is a way to get Internet at those stores for free, although the usual this-is-illegal-so-read-the-disclaimer-on-pages-149-and-150 applies.

1. There are three pieces of software you should download: **WireShark**, **Angry IP Scanner**, and **MAC Makeup**. The basic premise of paid wireless service is to give your credit card information to the company so that a certain amount of money can be deducted for a certain period of Internet use. The premise behind

getting free Internet is making your computer look like one of the computers that are or were on the network.

2. You can either use **Angry IP Scanner** to see what other computers are on the network, or use **WireShark** and capture some of the data being sent over the network. My preference is **Angry IP Scanner** because it's simpler. When using **Angry IP Scanner**, set the range of IP addresses you want to search through (by default, the range is 0.0.0.0 to 0.0.0.0; I recommend making the range 10.10.10.10 to 255.255.255.255). Keep in mind that the program will ping, or test, every IP in the range (for example, making the range 0.0.0.0 to 255.255.255.255 will make the program ping 0.0.0.1, 0.0.0.2, etc. up to 0.0.0.255, then go to 0.0.1.0, etc.) which may take a while.

3. Pick an IP address that you believe has or had Internet access, and copy down the corresponding MAC address.

4. Copy down your original MAC address by going to the Command Prompt in Windows, typing "ipconfig /all", and copying down all the information.

5. Using **MAC Makeup**, switch your MAC address to the one of the computer you sniffed before.

6. You should now have Internet access. You may

have to change your MAC address back to your original one when you're done, since you're effectively accepting any actions the other computer performs as yours. Additionally, your Internet connection may speed up and slow down randomly, and may even stop working based on the strain on the network at any given time. Nevertheless, you are guaranteed a fairly reliable connection most of time—plus, it's free. Note that if nobody is one the network or if you do not configure the programs correctly, you will not be able to access the Internet.

To download music off the Internet for free:

The iPod-iTunes duo is the most popular hardware-software couple in the music world, and the numerous downsides are not immediatcly apparent. In the age before mp3s, you would go out and buy CDs to play on a computer or CD player, thereby having a physical copy of your data. If you copied the music on the CD onto a computer and the music was lost through a hard drive crash, accidental deletion, or otherwise, you only had to retrieve the CD to retrieve the songs. If you lose the music you bought from iTunes and did not back them up on an external drive, your music is lost and Apple will not refund your money. The same rule applies if the music you downloaded is corrupted and cannot be played. Therefore, I am a strong advocate of free music and an advocate of music piracy.

The above statement is undoubtedly very radical, and downloading music illegally can almost certainly result in one's arrest if caught. Yet my words come from years of experience with lost music and watching millions of dollars spent to the mp3 business. I am not saying that artists do not deserve their money for making the music we love, but rather that the music industry as a whole exploits populations to buy mp3s at an overpriced rate and then demands that they download tracks again if they are lost or damaged. With the tracks being in an intangible form, anything can go wrong with them, and Apple especially did not change its policies even after its exploding popularity. In addition, Apple does not allow full track previews, so you cannot hear the music you buy until you download it, and if you don't like the tracks you cannot get a refund. These one-way deals result in millions of dollars blatantly *wasted* by the American public each year, and thus I will explain how to get music off the Internet for free. Please note that doing so is at your own risk, and that the author is not liable for any damage, harm, illegal activity, mass chaos, or hysteria caused. For more information, please refer to pages 149 and 150.

There are two ways you can get music off the

Internet for free: legally and illegally. If you choose the virtuous legal path, there are numerous sites that list music for download recorded by budding artists in all genres of music (for example, mp3.com). In order to download music illegally, follow the following directions.

Try any or all of the following methods:

1. Visit **Seeqpod** at www.seeqpod.com/

2. Type in the name of the song or artist you're looking for.

3. Double click on one of the songs on the left side of the window; the song will play.

4. To save the song in a playlist you can revisit when online, just create a free account and click the "Save As" button.

5. To save the song to your desktop, download the free **Audacity** program (http://audacity.sourceforge.net/)

6. Also download the **LAME mp3 encoder** (http://www-users.york.ac.uk/~raa110/audacity/lame.html) by clicking any link on the page.

7. Install **Audacity**.

8. Unzip the **LAME mp3 encoder** package to a location you remember (not the desktop).

9. Right click on the volume control button in the bottom right hand corner.

10. Click on the "Open Volume Control" option.

11. In the top left hand corner of the resulting window, click the "Options" button.

12. Click the "Properties" option in the resulting menu.

13. Click the "Recording" radio button that appears about a quarter way down from the top of the window.

14. Ensure that the only box checked towards the bottom of the screen in the one associated with "Wave Out Mix".

15. Click "OK".

16. The volume control button for "Wave Out Mix" should be the window showing at this point. Make the volume about three quarters high (one quarter of the way from full volume).

17. Click OK.

18. **Audacity** should be set up to use "Wave Out Mix". You can check by looking at the drop down menu that appears between the menu bar and the gray area in Audacity. If it does not say "Wave Out Mix", click on the drop down arrow and make it so.

19. Click the record button in **Audacity** and immediately switch to your Internet browser and begin playing the desired song.

20. When the song is done, click the stop button.

21. In **Audacity**, click on "File".

22. In the resulting menu, click either "Export to MP3" or "Export to WAV". If you export to mp3, direct Audacity to the location of the **LAME mp3 encoder** when it prompts you (it will only prompt you once, but you have to keep the location the same).

23. Your file will be saved to the location of your choice. An alternative to using Audacity is **FreeCorder** (http://www.freecorder.com/freecorder3/index.php?), a free web browser add-on that allows you to record music directly from the website. Download and install it, visit the website with the desired song, and **FreeCorder** will let you record the audio directly from the browser without interference from other system sounds.

1. Search for any website with full song previews. My favorites are **YouTube**, **Napster**, and **MOG**, but there are more. Note that when visiting the **Napster** homepage, you have to scroll to the

bottom and click on the "Click Here" link that appears next to the words "Not Ready to Get Napster?"in order to get to the free music page. If that link is not available on the bottom of the page, go to the website directly at http://free.napster.com/.

2. Find the song you want to play by searching on the sites.

3. Follow steps 5-23 above.

1. Visit the **G2P** website (www.g2p.org/).

2. Type in the name of the song or artist, or select one of the other options in the top right corner so you can look for videos, eBooks, software, and others.

3. On the resulting page, click on the first link.

4. If the resulting page contains other links, search for the name of the song or artist you were looking for in Firefox by holding the control button down and then clicking "F".

5. When the link containing the name is highlighted, click on it.

6. The music or video should play. Preview it and ensure it is what you want. If it is, go back one page, right click on the link, and select "Save Link As". The music will be saved to your

computer. If it is not what you were looking for, go back two pages to the Google search page, click on the next link, and repeat steps 4-6.

To share your wired Internet connection with others:

There are many instances where you may have access to a wired Internet connection, but others around you do not. If you find it in your heart to share the connection, you can follow the following steps on Mac OS X and Windows Vista and XP to turn your computer into what is essentially a router, allowing others to connect to your wireless hotspot and get a connection. You can even set a password for your hotspot; all you need is a computer that takes in a wired Internet connection and also has an ability to receive wireless connections.

Mac OS X

1. Go to "System Preferences".

2. Click on the "Sharing" button.

3. Click on the "Internet" tab.

4. Under "Share Your Connection From", select "Built-In Ethernet".

5. Under "To Computers Using", select "Airport".

6. Under "Options" you can enter a name and,

optionally, a password for your hotspot. Ensure that you choose the WEP encryption option if you enter a password.

7. Click the "Start" button.

Windows Vista

1. Go to the Control Panel.

2. Click on the "Network and Sharing Center" button.

3. Under "Tasks", choose "Set up a new connection".

4. Click the "Wireless Ad Hoc Network" button.

5. Enter a name, and, optionally, a password for your hotspot.

6. Click "Turn On Internet Connection Sharing".

Windows XP

1. Go to the Control Panel.

2. Open "Network Connections".

3. Right click "Wireless Connections" and click "Properties".

4. Under the "Wireless Networks" tab, ensure the "Use Windows to Configure my Wireless Network Settings" option is checked.

5. Under "Preferred Networks", click "Add".

6. Name your hotspot.

7. Under "Network Authentication", select "Shared".

8. Under Data Encryption, click "WEP" to enter a password or "Disabled" to make your hotspot accessible without a password.

9. Click "OK".

10. Click "Advanced".

11. Under "Networks to Access", click "Computer to Computer (Ad Hoc) Networks Only".

12. Click "OK".

13. Go back to "Network Connections".

14. Right click "Local Area Connection".

15. Click "Properties".

16. Click the "Advanced" tab.

17. Check the "allow Other Network Users to Control or Disable the Shared Internet Connection".

18. Click "OK".

19. See if the Internet is accessible through another computer. If it is not, the problem is most likely the existence of another setting located in your computer's setup. Restart your computer, and

look for the screen to display the word "Setup" or "BIOS". Note the key that is defined by those words. When your computer boots up, restart it again, continually pressing the aforementioned key. In the Setup menu, look for a setting that allows you to "Disable WiFi and Ethernet Switching", while at the same time making sure you do not change any of the other settings. Once you've disabled WiFi switching, save the settings and exit the BIOS.

Troubleshooting

What you should do if:

Your computer will not boot or start.

1. Make sure your computer is plugged in.

2. If you try to turn on the computer and it doesn't make any noise or lights, the power supply may need to be replaced.

3. If the computer does start but you do not see anything on the screen, the monitor may be damaged. Try plugging the monitor into another computer with a different monitor video cable to see if it works. If it works, the video cable may need to be replaced.

4. If none of the above is the problem, you may be

experiencing bad RAM, hard drive failure, or a damaged CPU or motherboard. In these cases, take the computer to a professional if you are not capable of doing repairs yourself or look online for more information; your data may or may not be damaged as well.

5. If Windows starts but doesn't work properly in regular mode, try booting it into safe mode by starting the computer and pressing the key that leads to the boot menu, and select safe mode. If that doesn't work, try selecting the "Use the Last Known Configuration" option in the boot menu. If you still have a problem, take the computer to a professional if you are unable to diagnose the problem yourself or look online for more information; your data may or may not be damaged as well.

Your computer is overwhelmed with popups:

1. You have a serious spyware or adware problem. First, download Ad-Aware (the latest free version is good) and SpyBot. Run both and let them find and take care of the problems.

2. If you still have a problem, download HijackThis. Let it do a scan of your computer, then upload the resulting file to the HijackThis forum. One of their advisors will then interpret

the file and tell you how to eradicate the problem.

3. If none of the above programs worked, try using System Restore to go back to a previous point in time on your computer. If the problem is still existent, you may have to reinstall your operating system.

Your Internet connection doesn't work:

1. Try connecting to the Internet on another machine to see if the problem is the Internet or your computer. If the problem is your computer, the wireless or network card may be damaged.

2. If the problem is the Internet, ensure all cables are properly plugged in and your wireless Internet connection is on (if you use it).

3. If the above doesn't work, try resetting your modem or router by turning your modem, router, and computer off, waiting thirty seconds, and then turning them back on.

4. If you usually connect with a wireless adapter, try connecting directly to the Internet via an Ethernet cable. If you can get a connection, the wireless adapter may be to blame. If you still cannot get a connection, call up your Internet provider, since there may be a problem on their

side.

You spilled liquid on your electronics:

1. Shut off all the electronics immediately and remove any external devices plugged into it (memory cards, flash drives, keyboards, etc.) Try to get as much moisture off the electronics as possible as quickly as possible.

2. Put the device in a bag with as many silica gel packets as you can find. If you don't have any, use uncooked white rice grains, or even salt, as they all absorb moisture (make sure not of the above actually enter the electronics and touch the components).

3. Put the electronics in the back of a car window for an hour (make sure the temperature doesn't go over 150 degrees Fahrenheit). Alternatively, you can put the electronics in your oven at about 120 degrees Fahrenheit for an hour.

4. If you got soda on the electronics, use a cotton swab dipped in 99% rubbing alcohol to wipe off as many of the touched components as possible.

You deleted an important file:

1. Stop all programs, especially those like Google's

Desktop search that index locations on your computer, disconnect from the Internet, and shut off the computer. Any programs that write or rearrange data on your hard drive (for example, Disk Defragment) may overwrite the file, diminishing any chance that you will recover it.

2. Use a good undelete program. My favorite is Diskeeper and ZAR, though there are other alternatives out there.

3. As a preventative measure, backup your files every night on an external drive, keeping at least four days' copies before deleting the oldest one.

Disclaimer

By purchasing this book the consumer agrees to the following conditions. Additionally, by reading this book the reader agrees to the following conditions:

The author of this book is not liable for any damages, lawsuits, or injury established by reading this book and/or performing the actions described therein. The products and services described in this book are the copyright and property of their respective owners, and it is not the responsibility of the author for any discontinuation or either warranted or unwarranted change in the products. The inclusion of any work in this book does not constitute an endorsement of any other work on behalf of the works' owners and all entities thereby associated. The author is not responsible for any guilt felt after buying a Mac. The author is not responsible for any money paid for software, hardware, or anything else that does not perform as described in this book, on the Internet, or elsewhere and otherwise. The author is not to be held responsible for any data or money lost as a result of the reader's following of the directions described in this book. Some of the actions described in this book are expressly illegal; it is therefore the reader's, not the author's, decision to complete the actions and therefore the reader, not the author, is responsible for any criminal activity performed. It is to be noted that it is the author's express right to describe *how* to perform illegal actions, and by doing so is not admitting himself in any way that he has performed such actions. Any and all of the above may or may not apply to any one person, and by stating the above the author is in no way predicting that any of the above will occur. The author is not responsible for any typographical errors found in this book. All of the above apply to the author as well as any entities directly associated with the book. It is the author's right to be able to change any and all of the conditions in this disclaimer at any point in time.

Notes:

www.ingramcontent.com/pod-product-compliance
Lightning Source LLC
Chambersburg PA
CBHW022057210326
41519CB00054B/570

* 9 7 8 0 6 1 5 1 6 1 8 4 6 *